THE
LEGACY
OF THE
BEAST

THE
LEGACY
OF THE
BEAST

The Life, Work and Influence
of Aleister Crowley

Gerald Suster

SAMUEL WEISER, INC.
York Beach, Maine

To Alwine

First American edition 1989 by
Samuel Weiser, Inc.
Box 612
York Beach, Maine 03910

Second printing, 1990

Photographs courtesy of the BBC Hilton Picture Library

Library of Congress Cataloging in Publication Data

Suster, Gerald.
    The legacy of the beast.

        Originally published: London: W.G. Allen, 1988.
        1. Crowley, Aleister, 1875-1947.   2. Authors,
English—20th Century— Biography.   3. Occultists
—Great Britain—Biography.   I. Title.
PR6005.R7Z88 1989   828'.91209 [B]   88-33891
ISBN 0-87728-697-3

Printed in the United States of America

Foreword

Those who have written at lesser or greater length upon the subject of Aleister Crowley have included the poet W.B. Yeats, who described him as 'an unspeakable lunatic', the bibliographer Timothy d'Arch Smith, who looks upon him as having been one of the most interesting book designers of his time, and the late Israel Regardie, chiropractor and psychotherapist, who thought Crowley was a spiritual genius.

Now Gerald Suster, no doubt a better chiropractor than Mr Timothy d'Arch Smith and a better poet than Israel Regardie, has joined the growing number of those who have expressed in print their reactions to Crowley's life and ideas.

There is no entry for Crowley, who died in 1947, in the relevant supplement to that monument of Victorian scholarship, the *Dictionary of National Biography*. This is perhaps as it should be; whatever his virtues may have been, Crowley would fit uneasily into the DNB. And yet, curiously enough, one of the—in every sense—weighty volumes of the DNB contains an entry devoted to a man who reminds me of Crowley.

The entry in question is concerned with an obscure Londoner who flourished in the 1670s—his dates of birth and death are unknown—and whose contemporaries referred to him as 'our modern Proteus'.

Proteus, of course, featured in the mythology of ancient Greece as a being who had the capacity to change his shape at will. The 'modern Proteus' of the London of Nell Gwynn, Rochester and Samuel Pepys was almost as versatile, having the ability to voluntarily dislocate every joint in his body. He employed this unusual talent to irritate his contemporaries.

On one occasion he summoned a noted surgeon and bone-setter—who became ill at the sight of the seeming deformities with which he was faced and had to be helped from the room. He drove an unfortunate tailor to the brink of hysteria by ordering a suit from him; at each supposedly final fitting the astonished tradesman would find

5

that, somehow or other, he had previously failed to notice that the coat should be tailored to accommodate a grossly hunched back, or that one of his client's legs was some five inches shorter than the other.

Crowley caused his tailors no problems, or at least none unconnected with the payment of bills, but he too was, in a sense, a Proteus—appearing to one man as a typical Englishman, to another as a poet of genius, to another as a master magician or a confidence trickster. I suspect that, like his forerunner of the seventeenth century, Crowley took a Puckish delight in the confusions born of his transformations.

Crowley's Proteus-like qualities have remained apparent over the forty years or so since his death—for almost everyone who has written about him has presented a different Crowley to the world. The late Louis Wilkinson's Crowley was a delightful friend and companion who held curious religious beliefs; Arthur Calder-Marshall's was a tiresomely boring old confidence trickster; Mr John Symonds' Crowley was a man who made a religion out of his personal weaknesses; Timothy d'Arch Smith's was a book designer, albeit one who practised magic.

In *The Legacy of the Beast* Gerald Suster gives us a Crowley who was, if I understand Mr Suster aright, both the Prophet of a New Dispensation and a Taoist sage. Crowley would have found this pleasing; he believed that he was a prophet and was sure that he was the only westerner who truly understood the inmost nature of Taoist doctrine. I feel that at times Mr Suster has been so captured by his image of 'Crowley as Taoist sage' that he has come close to writing a Taoist hagiography of the man who termed himself 'the Beast 666'. If *The Legacy of the Beast* was no more than that it might still be well worth reading.

The real importance of the book, however, lies not in its hagiographical element. Still less is it to be found in the almost seventeenth-century forthrightness with which Mr Suster expresses his opinions—by no means all of them shared by me—concerning others who have written about Crowley, the Hermetic Order of the Golden Dawn and similar subjects.

The essential virtue of *The Legacy of the Beast* is that it provides, for the first time, a clearly written and often amusingly presented account of the core of Crowley's teachings, theoretical and practical, which can be easily understood by the ordinary reader as well as by the occult specialist.

Mr Suster has written a book which should appeal to the man (or woman) in the street as well as to the specialist in esoteric studies. It is to be hoped that it will find, as it deserves to find, a place on many bookshelves.

Francis X. King

Preface

The list of books on occultism, and especially on Magic, grows each year, the bad ones far outnumbering the good. Yet there is one astonishing gap. A work which explains the ideas and influence of Aleister Crowley to the general reader is not to be found. This is remarkable: discussing occultism and the raising of consciousness without mentioning Crowley is rather like discussing the Second World War without mentioning Winston Churchill.

John Symonds' biography, *The Great Beast*, written over 35 years ago and the source from which so many have drawn their information, does not begin to deal with Crowley's ideas. It is dated in its Victorian attitudes and marred by prejudice, hostility, fictionalized sensationalism; by its refusal to expound the essence of Crowley's thought; and even by plain inaccuracy. A fresh approach is sorely needed for the eighties and after.

Although close on forty years have passed since Crowley's death, he commands widespread and growing attention. He has many more disciples now than in his lifetime and the number is increasing; the books which were once rare collectors' items are now constantly republished; he was recognized by the *Sunday Times* as among the 'One Thousand Makers of the Twentieth Century'; his *MAGICK in Theory and Practice* has become a book club title; and his name keeps cropping up on television (even on mountaineering programmes), radio broadcasts and rock music albums, in newspaper articles and during court proceedings. Whenever there is a court case involving 'black magic', Crowley's name is invariably cited. Reporters go back to old copies of the *Sunday Express* or *John Bull* and the same tired lies and fabrications are rehashed for popular consumption. Once again one reads shocking tales of sex, drugs and satanism, despite the fact that Crowley's use of sex and drugs would sound commonplace to the average rock star or Hollywood starlet and the man was not a satanist at all. Nevertheless, this legend of 'wickedness' has kept his name alive.

Perhaps the best known and least interesting facts about Crowley are that he enjoyed sex and took drugs. So what? If all he achieved consisted of indulging these appetites, parading in robes and upsetting the middle classes of his day, he is best forgotten. But those who look harder and deeper into the matter discover a man who belies this unsavoury legend.

Most people who disparage Crowley have not read his writings. Yet some of the millions who are interested in mysticism and the occult, and who buy books on the subject, find it uniquely refreshing to come upon Crowley, after the frustration of ploughing through volumes by charlatans and posers, for he is 'the real thing'. He is the clearest and most authoritative exponent of Magic(k) in theory and practice – and also of Yoga. Those who pursue the matter further discover a system for raising human consciousness, intelligence and potential which possesses great beauty and intellectual complexity. Crowley raises profound metaphysical issues and is thought by some to be the equal of the greatest mystics. To this must be added the religious aspect of Crowley as The Beast 666, Prophet of a New Aeon.

The purpose of this work is to investigate and answer questions of abiding interest. Who was this man who will not go away? What did he stand for? And what is all the fuss about? Why do people keep mentioning his name? To many, the whole business sounds somewhat peculiar and unpleasant. But what is the truth of the matter? Was Crowley anything more than a colourful figure of fun who won infamy through his excesses? Did he really have anything important to say to anyone? Why did the gutter press call him 'the wickedest man in the world' and 'a man we'd like to hang'? If he was indeed, (as he claimed) maligned, misjudged, misunderstood and vilified, why did he also claim to be The Beast 666? It is clear that Crowley devoted his life to his Magick—and what exactly is *that*?—but was he mad? Was he not simply creating a religion out of his own weakness? If so, why are people paying him more and more attention?

These issues must be tackled fairly and sensibly. Accordingly, this work will relate Crowley's life, consider his legend, present the man, examine his ideas and contemplate his legacy.

Author's Note

Footnotes are usually tiresome and, in a work of this nature, require a few words of apology and explanation. Their purpose is either to indicate the source of a disputed point of information or to comment further upon a controversial detail. I have tried to make them lively. But they are of interest primarily to the specialist, and can be cheerfully ignored by the general reader.

PART ONE

The Life

Select Chronology

1875	Born at Leamington Spa, Warwickshire on 12 October.
1887	His father, Edward Crowley, dies.
1895	Matriculation at Trinity College, Cambridge.
1896	First mystical experience.
1898	His first published poem, *Aceldama*.
	Meets Gerald Kelly.
	Leaves Cambridge.
	Meets George Cecil Jones and is initiated into the Hermetic Order of the Golden Dawn.
1899	Meets Allan Bennett and receives more intensive magical instruction.
	Meets the Chief of the Golden Dawn, 'MacGregor' Mathers.
	Acquires Boleskine House.
1900	Schism in the Golden Dawn.
	Mathers initiates Crowley into Adeptship in Paris.
	Crowley leaves for Mexico.
1901	Concentration exercises and mountaineering in Mexico with Oscar Eckenstein.
	Writes *Alice: An Adultery*.
	Sees Allan Bennett and studies and practises Yoga under him in Ceylon. Attains trance of Dhyana.
1901–2	Wanderings in India.
1902	Visits Bennett in Burma.
	Expedition to K2 led by Eckenstein.
	Arrives in Paris.
1903	Returns to Boleskine.
	Meets Rose Kelly, Gerald's sister, and marries her.
1903–4	Honeymoon travels to Paris, Naples, Cairo and India; return to Cairo.
1904	8–10 April: *The Book of the Law* dictated to Crowley.
1905–7	Publication of *The Collected Works of Aleister Crowley*.

13

1905	Expedition to Kangchenjunga.
1906	Travels through Southern China with Rose and daughter. Augoeides Invocations.
	Death of his daughter, Lilith.
	Attains Nirvikalpa Samadhi and completes Abra-Melin Operation.
	Writes *Seven Seven Seven*.
	Acknowledged as a Master by George Cecil Jones.
1907	Reception of *The Holy Books* commences.
	A∴A∴ founded.
	Friendship with Captain J.F.C. Fuller.
	Visits Morocco with the Earl of Tankerville.
1908	Walks across Spain and visits Morocco with Victor Neuburg.
	Performs 'John St. John' Operation in Paris.
1909–13	Publishes the first ten numbers of *The Equinox*.
1909	The A∴A∴ opened to new members.
	Finds missing manuscript of *The Book of the Law*.
	Rose divorces Crowley.
	The Vision and the Voice received in the Sahara with Victor Neuburg.
	Crowley formally accepts the exalted Grade of Master of the Temple.
1910	Meets Leila Waddell.
	The Rites of Eleusis performed at Caxton Hall.
1911	George Cecil Jones sues *The Looking Glass* for libel and loses. Jones, Fuller and others break with Crowley.
	Another visit to the Sahara with Neuburg.
	Writing of the major *Magical Instructions*.
	Meets Mary d'Este Sturges. The Abuldiz Working.
1912	*Book Four Parts 1 and 2* published as a result of the Abuldiz Working.
	Theodor Reuss initiates Crowley into the Ordo Templi Orientis and appoints him head of the British branch.
1913	Visit to Moscow with 'The Ragged Rag-Time Girls'. Writing of *Hymn to Pan, City of God* and *The Fun of the Fair*.
	The Book of Lies published.
1914	The Paris Working with Victor Neuburg.
	Departure for the United States.
1915	Work on *Astrology* with Evangeline Adams.
	Employed by Viereck to work on *The Fatherland*.
	Affair with Jeanne Foster, 'Hilarion' and 'The Cat'.
	Work with Charles Stansfield Jones in Vancouver.
	Crowley claims the Grade of Magus, Prophet of a New Aeon.
1916	Magical Retirement in New Hampshire.
	Period of despair in New Orleans.

14

1917	Becomes Editor of *The International*.
	Takes up painting.
1918	*Liber Aleph* completed.
	Amalantrah Working with Roddie Minor.
	Magical Retirement on Oesopus Island.
	Crowley's version of *Tao Teh King*.
	Meets Leah Hirsig.
1919	*The Blue Equinox*, Volume III, Number 1 published.
	Return to England with Leah.
	Inheritance of £3000.
1920	Abbey of Thelema founded in Cefalu, Sicily.
	Anne Leah (Poupeé), daughter of Crowley and Leah, dies.
	Ninette Shumway at Abbey; Jane Wolfe arrives.
1921	Crowley claims the Supreme Grade of Ipsissimus but swears never to divulge the fact.
	Mary Butts and Cecil Maitland visit the Abbey; so do C.F. Russell and Frank Bennett.
1922	Publication of *Diary of a Drug Fiend*.
	New campaign of newspaper assaults on Crowley.
1923	Raoul Loveday dies at Cefalu.
	Crowley expelled from Italy by Mussolini.
	Arrival in Tunis and completion of *The Confessions*.
1924	The 'Supreme Ordeal' in Paris.
	Meets Dorothy Olsen and goes with her to North Africa.
1925	The 'World Teacher' campaign launched.
	Invited by Herr Traenker to Thuringia in Germany to become International Head of the OTO.
1926–8	Travels in France, Germany and North Africa.
1928	Israel Regardie joins Crowley in Paris and becomes his Secretary.
1929	Crowley, Regardie and Crowley's mistress, Maria Teresa de Miramar, expelled from France. Crowley returns to England. *Magick: in Theory and Practice* published in Paris and London.
	Crowley marries Maria in Germany.
1930	First two volumes of *The Confessions* published.
1930–4	Wanderings in Germany and Portugal.
1932	Regardie and Crowley part company.
1934	Crowley loses his libel case against Nina Hamnett and Constable & Co. over *Laughing Torso*.
1935	Crowley made bankrupt.
1936–8	Visits to Germany.
1937	Publication of *The Equinox of the Gods*.
1939	Publication of *Eight Lectures on Yoga*.
	Suggests 'V' Sign to the Foreign Office.

1940	Publication of *Thumbs Up!*
1944	Publication of *The Book of Thoth* with Tarot cards painted by Lady Frieda Harris.
1945	Crowley retires to 'Netherwood', Hastings and works on *Magick Without Tears*.
1947	1 December: Crowley dies at Hastings.
	5 December: 'The Last Ritual' and cremation at Brighton.

1

Material on Crowley's life is so abundant that an industrious author and scholar could easily write a million words on the subject. Crowley's autobiography consists of six volumes comprising 923 printed pages in one edition, yet ends in 1923 when there were twenty-four more years of bizarre happenings, productive work, enduring achievements and salacious scandals to follow. There are at least six biographies, the quality of which varies from the splendid to the silly.[1] There are many volumes of memoirs and studies of the period,[2] which include interesting information, perceptions, myths, legends, truths and lies about him. Above all else, there is a vast quantity of diaries, letters, unpublished manuscripts and other documentation, keenly collected, zealously preserved and judiciously annotated by the late Gerald Yorke in the Yorke Collection at the Warburg Institute of the University of London.[3]

However, it is not my intention to probe into the question of whether, at 4.00 pm on 6 June 1921, Aleister Crowley had tea or coffee (though thorough research could probably ascertain the nature of the disputed beverage). My purpose here is simply to give a straightforward account of his extraordinary life.

Aleister Crowley was born Edward Alexander Crowley between 11.00 pm and midnight on 12 October, 1875, at Leamington Spa, Warwickshire. His father, Edward Crowley,[4] was a wealthy retired brewer. His mother, Emily Bertha Bishop, came from a Devon and Somerset family. Both parents were Plymouth Brethren—an extreme Christian sect, founded by

John Nelson Darby, which insists on the literal interpretation of the Bible as the exact words of the Holy Ghost.

The religious fanaticism of Edward Crowley led him to spend much of his time preaching the Word. He went on walking tours throughout England, evangelized in every town and engaged perfect strangers in conversation. One of his favourite ploys was to ask a man what he was doing and to respond to the answer with: 'And then?' The man would continue. 'And then?' This would go on until the man said something like: 'Well, and then I'll die, I suppose.' Edward Crowley would gaze at him gravely as he demanded solemnly: 'And *then?*' The answer to this and all other problems was contained in his oft-repeated slogan: 'Get right with God!' The preacher would exhort his interlocutor to faith in Jesus and the virtues of Bible study, extract his address and for years afterwards, send him free religious tracts.

His son loved and respected him. 'My father, wrong-headed as he was,' he wrote years later, 'had humanity and a certain degree of common-sense.' Inspired by his father's faith, the child Crowley was a fervent little Plymouth Brother who studied the Bible eagerly. He was particularly fascinated by the prophetic passages in *Revelation* forecasting the appearance of The Beast 666 and the Scarlet Woman. He imagined himself to be a servant of God who was only too ready and willing to crusade against Satan and his hordes. Yet from an early age one can detect a mischievous sense of humour. When he was told not to grimace because he might be 'stuck like that', he gazed thoughtfully at the Plymouth Brethren around him and replied: 'So that accounts for it.'

Although Christmas was forbidden as a pagan festival and life in the Crowley household was ruled by the words of the Bible, the child was not unhappy until the death of his father on 5 March 1887. Although he never revealed when the sentiment first arose, he came to dislike his mother intensely, writing: 'her powerful natural instincts were suppressed by religion to the point that she became, after her husband's death, a brainless bigot of the most narrow, logical and inhuman type.' It seems that she tried to make a sanctimonious prig out of her son and when this intention failed, she retaliated by calling him 'The Beast'.

After Edward Crowley's death, much time was spent in the London household of the boy's maternal uncle, Tom Bishop, of whom he wrote: 'No more cruel fanatic, no meaner villain, ever walked this earth.' Bishop's narrow and petty ways extended to forbidding *David Copperfield* to the young Crowley because it contained a character called Emily; his mother's name was Emily and the prose of Dickens might cause the boy to disrespect his mother. But Bishop's tyranny appears mild by comparison with that of the Reverend H.d'Arcy Champney, who ran a school for the sons of Brethren in Cambridge. Crowley called his time there 'A Boyhood In Hell'.

The school was cruel, sadistic and fanatical. One boy was convicted of some petty theft of which he was innocent and sentenced to one hundred and twenty strokes of the cane on his bare shoulders. Nor did Crowley escape corporal punishment: 'I remember one licking I got—on the legs, because flogging the buttocks excites the victim's sensuality!—fifteen minutes prayer, fifteen strokes of the cane, fifteen minutes more prayer, fifteen more strokes—and more prayer to top it!' Matters grew worse. The boy was one day told to confess to some unspeakable crime. No specific accusation was made. Yet

> I was put into 'Coventry', i.e. no master nor boy might speak to me or I to them. I was fed on bread and water; during play hours I worked in the schoolroom; during work hours I walked solitary round and round the playground . . . This punishment, which I believe criminal authorities would consider severe on a prisoner, went on for a term and a half . . . Physically, I broke down. The strain and misery affected my kidneys; and I had to leave school altogether for two years.

It is hardly suprising that Crowley came to loathe, abhor and despise Christianity. For a time, his health was so wretched that doctors feared he would die in his teens. When he was finally sent to Malvern, his physical weakness made him the target for every bully:

> They soon found me out! This kidney weakness causes

depression and physical cowardice, and the other boys were not sympathetic about kidneys, regarding them mostly as satisfactory parts of the body to punch.

Imagine my misery! The most powerful of all my passions—bar sloth—is Pride; and here was I, the object of universal contempt.

His health broke down again. He had to leave Malvern and private tutors were engaged. The boy might be a sickly wimp; but at least he was very intelligent for his age. He coped ably with all his studies and displayed a particularly strong interest in the Natural Sciences. He had definite talent for writing verse and also for chess. But perhaps his most important characteristic was the will to conquer his bodily deficiencies. In later life, he looked back gratefully on one tutor, an Oxford man called Archibald Douglas, who introduced him to smoking, drinking, racing, billiards, betting, cards and women.

I immediately accepted his standpoint and began to behave like a normal, healthy human being. The nightmare world of Christianity vanished at the dawn... For the first time in my life I was brought into contact with my fellow men and women. For the first time honest friendship, wholesome love, frank, gay and courageous, became possible and actual.

It was also at this period that the teenage Crowley took a more important step. He started on rock-climbing because it was the most dangerous of sports. The exercise hardened his body, toughened his mind and gave him genuine self-confidence. Soon he was regarded as a climber to watch: and alone among the peaks of the Lake District, he experienced a greater sense of freedom than any he had known. Soon he was fit enough to be sent to Tonbridge. Although he disliked the school, he was now impossible to bully. Curiously enough, he had to leave once more and again it was for health reasons—this time because he had 'caught the clap from a prostitute in Glasgow'.

It must have been the emergence of his sex-drive that prompted his outraged mother to call him 'The Beast'. His first experience appears to have been with a theatre girl in Torquay when he was sixteen.[5] Soon after, he seduced a maid in his mother's bedroom in a symbolic affirmation of rebellion, manhood and independence. As he grew, he flagrantly rejected the gloom, mediocrity and intolerance in which the Bishop family stewed, taking joy in the world of the senses and coming to perceive Jesus as the embodiment of the sin-complex and its attendant ills of oppression, meanness, cruelty and the passion to persecute.

There was little that his mother or his uncle could do about this. Crowley was due to inherit a sum of between thirty and forty thousand pounds, worth at least ten times as much by the standards of today. He took a perverse delight in shocking his family and blithely ignored all admonitions. Meanwhile, his reputation as a cragsman grew. He performed well in the Lake District and the Alps, then distinguished himself on the chalk cliffs of Beachy Head by succeeding with routes which have never been attempted before or since. It was said that he *oozed* over rocks.

In October 1895, Crowley went up to Trinity College, Cambridge and 'found myself suddenly in an entirely new world. I was part of the glories of the past; and I made a firm resolution to be one of the glories of the future.' The bare official record tells us little: he took the second part of the General Examination in the Michaelmas Term 1896, the first part in the Easter Term 1897; he passed the Special Examination in Chemistry with a second class the following Michaelmas Term; and he left after the Easter Term 1898 without bothering to take a degree. This undistinguished academic record hardly tells the full story. Many have found their period at Cambridge or Oxford University to be the most intense experience of their lives. Whilst this was not the case with Crowley, whose adventures began, rather than ended, there, these years were nevertheless vital to his future development.

His general attitude was characterized by a haughty independence, which he emphasized by changing his name. He had read that the most favourable name for becoming famous was one consisting of a dactyl followed by a spondee: like 'Anthony

Bedser'. Since his middle name was Alexander and Aleister is its Gaelic form, he became Aleister Crowley; though he continued to pronounce the family name as in 'holy'. He declined to dine in Hall with his fellow-undergraduates because the timing did not suit him; and he had his meals sent up to his rooms from the Trinity kitchens. Chapel was then obligatory but he refused to attend. With forked tongue sticking maniacally through each cheek, he excused himself on the grounds that he had been brought up among the Plymouth Brethren, writing to the junior dean that 'the seed planted by my father, watered by my mother's tears, would prove too hardy a growth to be uprooted even by his eloquence and learning.' He followed a time-honoured tradition in rarely going to lectures and neglecting his designated studies: and his tutor, Dr Verrall, followed an equally long and honourable tradition in leaving him alone.

In fact, Crowley was studying furiously. He had come to realize how shamefully ill-read he was and so he now devoured everything important in the English language with the utmost thoroughness. He also read French literature and the major Greek and Latin classics. He bought books 'literally by the ton' and thought it disgraceful to leave them unread. By 1898, books covered his walls to the ceiling and filled four revolving bookshelves. There were many volumes on science, philosophy and even on alchemy. 'Nothing else seemed to me worthwhile but a thorough reading of the great minds of the past ... It was very rare that I got to bed before daylight.'

Yet he also found time for recreation in canoeing, cycling and, whenever he visited London, ice-skating. For further intellectual exercise there was chess, which he studied and practised for over four hours a day with the intention of becoming world champion. By his second year at Cambridge, he had been awarded his half-Blue and become president of the chess club. He defeated first-rate amateurs and the future champion of Scotland and was regarded as a coming master.

As for social life, 'I was surrounded by a more or less happy, healthy, prosperous set of parasites.' In an economic sense, Crowley was a parasite too. He spent freely on whatever took his fancy, and as he later admitted, his upbringing had left him hopelessly ill-educated in matters of sensible money-management. He had been taught to expect every possible material comfort as a right for which his family paid, yet until now had been kept very short of pocket money for his own use. As a result, his attitude to money remained unbalanced throughout his life. Extremely generous with whatever he had, he nevertheless quarrelled with tradesmen over petty sums: a proverbial case of 'penny wise, pound foolish'. Yet as his friend Louis Wilkinson would write: 'He treated his fortune as a toy. If you fit out mountaineering expeditions and are continually printing sumptuous private editions of your poems and plays and magical works, and buying places in Scotland, and living everywhere like a prince and entertaining like a Maharajah, even a large fortune won't last very long. But what *panache*, what *élan* and *brio* while it does last!'[6]

Politically, he was a staunch Tory and this stance was vividly coloured by right-wing romanticism. He joined a futile conspiracy to restore Don Carlos to the Spanish throne and claimed he had been knighted for his services.[7] He also joined a society called The Celtic Church, undertook the vigil required for initiation and temporarily praised the virtue of knightly chastity. However, the truth about his sex-life was rather different from his proclaimed ideals. His wealth gave him entry to the poor and willing girls of the town. 'I found even forty-eight hours of abstinence sufficient to dull the fine edge of my mind.' Of course this does not mean that throughout his time at Cambridge he had a woman every two days. He once wrote of 'The stupidity of having had to waste uncounted priceless hours in chasing what ought to have been brought to the back door every evening with the milk!'

During the vacations, he added to his growing reputation as a daring mountaineer with impressive climbs in the Alps, including a solitary ascent of the Eiger. But there were other travels too. His ambition was to join the Diplomatic Service and so he visited St. Petersburg, now Leningrad. He also travelled alone in Scandinavia and Holland, recording his impressions in the poems subsequently published as *Songs of the Spirit*.

It was in Stockholm on New Year's Eve 1896 that he

underwent his first mystical experience—something of which he tells us little: 'I was awakened to the knowledge that I possessed a magical means of becoming conscious of and satisfying a part of my nature which had up to that moment concealed itself from me. It was an experience of horror and pain, combined with a certain ghostly terror, yet at the same time it was the key to the purest and holiest spiritual ecstasy that exists.' In October 1897, there occurred a second experience which he defined rather more clearly and it was one which many have undergone. Its nature and its significance to Western Man have been brilliantly explored, for instance, by Colin Wilson in *The Outsider*. The Outsider is the one 'who sees too deep and too much', becoming, in consequence, alienated from the herd and its material concerns; for he is appalled by the futility of all human endeavour. Buddhists call this the Trance of Sorrow. Others might term it 'an existential crisis'. All who have experienced it agree on three points: the feeling is one of bitter agony; eventually one becomes conscious of a ravenous hunger and infinite yearning—suspected in themselves to be futile—for some secret glory which will restore essential meaning to life; and it changes one's fundamental point of view for a lifetime.

These were the effects upon the young Crowley. A career in diplomacy now seemed utterly pointless to him. Though he would continue to play chess well until he died, he lost his ambition to become an international master. Instead he sought feverishly for a metaphysical solution to the most profound and deeply painful problem he had hitherto encountered. In the cultural context of the late 1890s, this was no easy task. The few Westerners who brought acute scrutiny to bear upon perplexing questions were not especially well advised by the writings of their contemporaries.

For instance, In Huysmans' *Down There*, the work which together with the same author's *Against Nature* inspired the French and English Decadent Movement, two sadly limited alternatives were proposed to materialism: Catholicism or Satanism. In common with many leading French, German and English artists, Crowley went through a 'satanic' phase whilst at the same time being attracted by Christian purity—and he suffered guilt on account of their utter incompatibility. He became further involved in the Decadent Movement as a result of meeting Herbert Charles Jerome Pollitt and falling in love with him.

Pollitt was a Cambridge MA, ten years older than Crowley, though he often returned to the Footlights Dramatic Club as a dancer and female impersonator; in this guise he called himself Diane de Rougy after the celebrated Liane de Pougy. More importantly, he was a friend of the leading decadent artist and illustrator, Aubrey Beardsley. Crowley's *Confessions* confess little about the nature of their relationship and here he is uncharacteristically coy; however, the work was published at a time when homosexuality was regarded as criminal, perverted and disgusting. The plain facts, as revealed in unpublished manuscripts, are that 'I lived with him as his wife' and he 'made a poet out of me'.

Crowley's confused quest for truth and wisdom beyond the material produced his first published poem: *Aceldama: A Place to Bury Strangers In—A Philosophical Poem* by 'A Gentleman of the University of Cambridge'. The short Preface displays his continuing obsession with dualism: 'God and Satan fought for my soul those three long hours. God conquered—now I have only one doubt left—which of the twain was God? Howbeit, I aspire!' The poem, which derives its style from Baudelaire and Swinburne, is about the agonizing struggles of a human soul in its search for God.

> I have discovered God! His ghastly way
>   Of burning ploughshares for my naked feet
>   Lies open to me—shall I find it sweet
> To give up sunlight for that mystic day
>   That beams its torture, whose red banners beat
>   Their radiant fire
> Into my shrivelled head, to wither Love's desire?

It was this work which led the young Gerald Kelly, who would later become President of the Royal Academy and receive a knighthood, to seek out the fellow undergraduate who had suddenly burst into song; Kelly and Crowley became firm friends. And it was during this time that Crowley pursued research into Magic as a means of overcoming his perplexities of soul. He had bought A.E. Waite's compilation, *The Book of Black Magic and of Pacts:* a fatuous work, as he would later admit, suited to the mentality of superstitious peasants. But the glamour of Black Magic has often excited the credulity of the young and foolish. What stimulated Crowley was Waite's hint that he knew of a Hidden Church which preserved the secrets of initiation, and he wrote to him.

Although Waite was a humourless and pompous pedant who posed as a scholar, wrote execrable prose and was terrified by the practical aspects of matters on which he pronounced so solemnly, he did perform the service of making valuable texts available and wrote a courteous reply to Crowley's enquiry, advising him to read *The Cloud upon the Sanctuary* by Councillor von Eckartshausen. Here Crowley learned of a secret community of saints who possessed every spiritual grace and held the keys of initiation, being active in the world and constituting an interior church behind the exterior, a Secret Sanctuary which preserves all the sacred mysteries of God and Nature. He promptly appealed with all his being to these saints, wherever they were, to take notice of him and assist his quest for their company. He cried to God to send him a Master. He undertook a furious course of reading and tried magical experiments without real success. He vowed to devote all that he had and all his faculties to becoming worthy of entry to the Secret Sanctuary. As a result of his intense aspiration, his relationship with Pollitt deteriorated. The latter had no sympathy with Crowley's quest and Crowley came to perceive their liaison as being incompatible with religious dedication. Although he would subsequently regret the fact, there was an irrevocable breach shortly after Crowley left Cambridge.

Like Byron, Shelley, Swinburne and Tennyson, he went down without taking a degree, for he could not see how it could benefit his aspirations: 'I was white-hot on three points; climbing, poetry and Magick.' The climbing had led that Easter to meeting a man Crowley would admire intensely for the rest of his life: Oscar

Eckenstein. Eckenstein was twenty years older and possibly the finest mountaineer in England. The two men climbed together and earned one another's respect. Eckenstein taught Crowley all he had learned of the climber's craft, and nor was his influence confined to mountaineering. 'Eckenstein's moral code was higher and nobler than that of any other man I have met,' Crowley wrote, adding that 'he made a man of me.'

Yet Crowley was by now a formidable mountaineer in his own right. According to Dr T.G. Longstaff, President of the Alpine Club 1947-9, he was 'a fine climber, if an unconventional one. I have seen him go up the dangerous and difficult right (true) side of the great ice fall of the Mer de Glace below the Géant alone, just for a promenade. Probably the first and perhaps the only time this mad, dangerous and difficult route had been taken.'[8] This recognition by a leading member of the Alpine Club came in 1950 and was somewhat belated, for during the 1890s and after, there was bitter hostility between the Club and Crowley. The issue was that of guides. Crowley did without them and claimed that most Alpine clubmen simply paid locals to haul them up a few well-known peaks. He attacked Club members for laziness, cowardice, ineptitude, jealousy and bad sportsmanship and they responded by ignoring his feats.

In between scaling peaks, poetry poured from his pen. *Aceldama* was followed by *The Tale of Archais, Songs of the Spirit,* and *Jephthah: A Tragedy*; also a curious volume called *White Stains.* This last, Crowley claimed, is a poetic refutation of von Krafft-Ebing's *Psychopathia Sexualis*, in which it is argued that sexual aberrations are the result of disease. Whether or not this was the intention, *White Stains* reads rather more like a collection of smutty adolescent verses with a Naughty Nineties flavour, though here and there one finds a tuneful melody and a pleasant, mild eroticism.

He continued his search for the Secret Sanctuary. In the Summer of 1898, Crowley was in a Zermatt beer hall where he fell into conversation with one Julian L. Baker, an analytical chemist. Crowley started to pontificate on alchemy only to realize in due course that Baker knew far more about it than he did. Could this be the Master for whom he had appealed? The next day, Crowley pursued him, renewed the acquaintanceship, told Baker of his search for the Secret Sanctuary and for a Master, and convinced him of his desperate sincerity. In reply, Baker hinted that he knew of an Assembly which might be what Crowley was seeking; as for a Master, he could at least effect an introduction to one who was a far greater magician than himself. Back in London, Baker kept his word and Crowley met George Cecil Jones whose 'spirit was both ardent and subtle' and who 'bore a striking resemblance to many conventional represent-ations of Jesus Christ'. Crowley was impressed by him, sat at his feet and learned all he could from him. Like Baker, Jones was an analytical chemist and (again in common with Baker) a member of a magical organization, the Hermetic Order of the Golden Dawn.

What is Magic? And what was the Golden Dawn? How was Magic practised within its portals? These matters will be tackled in greater depth in Part 3. A simple sketch will suffice for our present purposes. Magic is a way of perfecting the various faculties of Man and raising him in stages to Godhead; one might call it the Yoga of the West. In the course of performing it, the magician gains understanding of various subtle processes of Nature and comes into contact with beings who may or may not exist independently of the unconscious mind. It is argued by magicians that everything in the Universe is connected with everything else in an ordered pattern of correspondences. The paraphernalia employed in magical rituals—the circle, triangle, wands, cups, swords, disks, robes, incenses, words etc.—these are means of manipulating correspondences, enflaming the imagin-ation and focusing the will into a blazing stream of pure energy. Although branches of Magic deal with practical, material matters, the fundamental goal is the attainment of super-consciousness, enabling the magician to know and accomplish his true purpose in life. This is the High Magic to which the Golden Dawn Order was dedicated.

The origins of the Order are still a matter for dispute.[9] However, no one doubts that it was founded on the basis of a set of cipher manuscripts. These came into the possession of Dr W. Wynn Westcott, a London coroner, in 1887. Westcott asked an occult scholar, S.L. 'MacGregor' Mathers, to assist him. The code was contained in *Polygraphiae* by John Trithemius and the manuscripts turned out to contain skeletonic rituals of a loosely Rosicrucian nature and the address of one Fraulein Sprengel in Nuremberg. Westcott claimed that he wrote to her, receiving in return a Charter to found the Golden Dawn.

It has been alleged that Sprengel never existed and that Westcott was a fantasizing forger. But the controversy surrounding the Order's origins is not germane here. The facts remain that Mathers expanded and wrote up the skeletonic rituals and these were duly enacted in Temples set up in London, Edinburgh, Bradford, Weston-super-Mare and, later, Paris.

In 1891, Westcott claimed that Sprengel had died and her associates had broken off all communication, urging the Golden Dawn leaders to form their own links with 'the Secret Chiefs', allegedly superhuman beings concerned with the spiritual welfare of mankind. In Paris in 1892, Mathers claimed to have established these links. A second, inner and 'Rosicrucian' Order was founded, The Red Rose and the Cross of Gold, and page after page of theoretical and practical occult teaching flowed from the clairvoyantly inspired pen of Mathers. Interestingly enough, the resulting system was beautiful and possessed bewildering yet logically coherent complexity. For Mathers had welded together an amalgam of traditions drawn from the Magic of Egypt and Chaldea, the Hebrew Qabalah, the Tarot and Medieval and Renaissance esotericism with his own inspiration, into a body of knowledge and a method for practical utilization of that knowledge.

The Golden Dawn was divided into a series of Grades corresponding to the qabalistic Tree of Life. After attaining to the fifth Grade of Philosophus, one entered the Portal of the Inner Order and became eligible for initiation into Adeptship. There were three main Grades of Adeptship: Adeptus Minor, Adeptus Major and that held by Mathers, Adeptus Exemptus. Beyond this, there was a third Inner Order and this was the province of the Secret Chiefs themselves.

On 18 November 1898, Aleister Crowley was initiated into the Grade of Neophyte. He was absolutely serious and even asked

Jones whether people died during the ceremony. The ritual was beautiful and moving and Crowley took as his new magical name *Perdurabo*, which means 'I will endure'. Unfortunately, disappointment ensued. Brother Perdurabo had been sworn to total secrecy on pain of the most fearful penalties—and the Hebrew alphabet was now confided to his safe-keeping. He had expected that his fellow-members would be great Saints and Magi: in fact most of them were perfectly ordinary people he snobbishly dismissed as nonentities. There were actually some notable initiates who may not have been present on that occasion: W.B. Yeats, the poet; Arthur Machen and Algernon Blackwood, the writers; Florence Farr, actress and intimate of Bernard Shaw; Maud Gonne, who inspired Yeats; and Mrs Oscar Wilde.

Crowley expressed his misgivings to Jones and Baker. They urged him to concentrate on mastering the groundwork, and on rising through the Grades to the Second Order, before venturing to criticize matters which he had yet to understand. So he bowed to their wisdom, continued to learn from Jones and made rapid progress, taking the Zelator grade in December, Theoricus in January and Practicus in February. If his opinion of the majority of members did not markedly improve, he did become increasingly impressed by the Golden Dawn system and by its Chief.

S.L. 'MacGregor' Mathers, known in the Order as Deo Duce Comite Ferro, fascinated Crowley. For the impressionable young aspirant, he was the prototype of The Magician. No member could doubt Mathers' zeal, his sincerity or his magical abilities. Although he suffered from poverty and neglect, his belief in his mission — that he was the messenger and servant of the Secret Chiefs—was absolute. His resulting autocratic manner did not worry Crowley but it was already causing problems within the Order which would have serious repercussions.

When Crowley was not studying the magic arts as Brother Perdurabo, he was leading an interesting life as a wealthy young man-about-town called Count Vladmir Svareff. The adoption of these guises would be a lasting preoccupation. He was intrigued by the effects of these roles on others and also on himself. As Svareff he took a flat in Chancery Lane, furnished a magical

Temple within it, published lavish editions of poetry at his own expense, wined and dined well and led an active bisexual life which would in time scandalize certain members of the Golden Dawn. He saw friends like Oscar Eckenstein and Gerald Kelly and persuaded Kelly to join the Order. Although the friendship between Crowley and Kelly was based primarily on their love of art and intellectual communion, there exists a postcard from the former to the latter which Crowley has signed 'Maud', a possible indication that there was some physical intimacy.

Crowley's notions of women were at this period sadly typical of one with his upbringing. In his poetry, he either idealized them as pure goddesses or else perceived them as cruel demons of terrifying sexual power and rapacity—a fairly standard manifestation of the Oedipus complex. In his behaviour, he was gripped by a desire to 'find' himself through women and so had a number of affairs without falling in love.

His poetry met with mixed reactions from reviewers. *Songs of the Spirit*, for example, was condemned by *The Athenaeum*: 'We cannot say that these verses deserve to be read'; yet the *Manchester Guardian* called it 'a little book of unusual quality'. One evening, Crowley called on W.B. Yeats with the page proofs of *Jephthah*. 'He forced himself to utter a few polite conventionalities... But it would have been a very dull person indeed who failed to recognise the black, bilious rage that shook him to the soul... What hurt him was the knowledge of his own incomparable inferiority.' Fifteen years later, Yeats wrote that he thought Crowley insane but that he had 'written about six lines, amid much bad rhetoric, of real poetry'. Perhaps the fairest summary of Crowley's work at this time is that of Martin Booth: 'He wrote in a rhetorical, stylized, and often flowery manner best befitting the poets of the 1890s, and yet he looked forward to the twentieth century in that he tackled themes and concepts that were yet to become common poetic currency.'[10]

But the prime preoccupation was Magic and in the Spring of 1899, Crowley finally met his Guru. This was Allan Bennett, known in the Golden Dawn as Iehi Aour and esteemed second only to Mathers himself. Bennett was at that time living in poverty and squalor. Crowley invited him to share his Chancery

Lane flat and later called his mind 'pure, piercing and profound beyond any other in my experience'. This judgement was endorsed by Clifford Bax, who would meet Bennett in the 1920s and who fortunately recorded the conversation of this remarkable man.[11] As far as Crowley was concerned, only Oscar Eckenstein could be compared with Bennett. Two of Bennett's essays 'A Note on Genesis' and 'The Training of the Mind', are irrefutable testimony to the quality of his intelligence.

Bennett tutored Crowley in applied Qabalah and advanced ceremonial magic: the invocation of Gods, the evocation of spirits and the consecration of talismans. Unfortunately, the tutor suffered from ill-health, especially asthma, which he could relieve only through the ingestion of drugs. His experience with these convinced Bennett that they were worthy of investigation as vehicles for the expansion of consciousness and, with Crowley, he conducted a series of scientific experiments which would later bear full fruit in Crowley's brilliant essay, 'The Psychology of Hashish'.

In May, Crowley took his Philosophus grade. Although he was eager to proceed to the Second Order, the rule was that there must be an interval of at least seven months and that one had to be specially invited. Now he turned his attention to *The Book of the Sacred Magic of Abra-Melin the Mage*. This is easily the most impressive of the medieval grimoires. The Magician requires a house where he will not be disturbed. For six months he then aspires with increasing fervour and concentration to obtaining the Knowledge and Conversation of the Holy Guardian Angel. Once success is obtained, the Magician knows his true purpose in the world. He must now evoke the Four Great Princes of the Evil of the World, their eight sub-princes, and the 316 servitors which will charge previously prepared talismans, and these will enable the Magician to gratify his needs and desires. This grimoire, discovered by Mathers, had a sinister reputation. As Crowley wrote: 'The demons connected with *Abra-Melin* do not wait to be evoked; they come unsought,' and strange events began to occur. On one occasion, for instance, Crowley and Jones 'observed that semi-materialized beings were marching around the main room in almost unending procession'.

32

Bennett's health deteriorated until Jones and Crowley became convinced that he would die unless he went to live in a warmer climate. After a magical operation to evoke the Spirit Buer, whose function is to heal the sick, Bennett was presented with the necessary funds to enable him to sail for Ceylon.[12] Crowley now left London and purchased Boleskine House on the shores of Loch Ness, where he dedicated himself to the performance of the Abra-Melin Operation. It was clear to him that Jones and Bennett were right and he possessed all the talents necessary to become a great Magician. He made particular progress in astral vision and travel. However, his Operation was disrupted by the revolt which had broken out in the Golden Dawn.

The London members had grown weary of the dictatorship of Mathers, who for some years had been living in Paris with his wife Moina, sister of the philosopher Henri Bergson. A number of issues were involved, most of them beyond the scope of this work. But one was Brother Perdurabo. Towards the end of 1899 the London officers of the Second Order refused Crowley the Adeptus Minor initiation to which he was formally entitled. 'A mystical fraternity is not a moral reformatory,' Yeats commented acidly. Crowley went to Paris and presented his case to Mathers. Although the latter had never consummated his own marriage, he regarded a member's sex-life as being entirely his own affair—a major issue on which he clashed with certain London members—and initiated Perdurabo into Adeptship on 16 January 1900. The London rebels responded by refusing to give Crowley official copies of the instructional manuscripts to which he was entitled. Letters were exchanged between London and Paris and accusations were hurled until, at the end of March, the London Temple declared its independence of its creator. Crowley dashed back to Paris and pledged his loyalty to Mathers, returning to London as the latter's Envoy Plenipotentiary.

There occurred a magical duel between Yeats and Crowley, succinctly recorded by Francis King and Isabel Sutherland in their delightful history, *The Rebirth of Magic:*

[Yeats] claimed that the Order wonder-workers had 'called up' one of Crowley's mistresses on the astral plane and told her to betray her lover. Two days later, said Yeats, she spontaneously approached a member of the Order and offered to go to Scotland Yard and give evidence of 'torture and medieval iniquity'. Crowley's diary gave quite a different account of this psychic attack—his ornamental Rose Cross turned white, while fires refused to burn in his lodgings; his rubber mackintosh spontaneously went up in flames, for no apparent reason he lost his temper, and on at least five occasions horses bolted at the sight of him.

Crowley replied by seizing the Order's premises with the aid of some toughs he had hired at a pub in Leicester Square... The triumph was only a temporary one. With the aid of the police the Second Order regained control of its premises and, for good measure, managed to persuade one of Crowley's creditors to issue a writ against him.

While all this was going on in London Mathers was resorting to black magic in Paris. He had taken a large packet of dried peas, baptised each pea with the name of one of his opponents, invoked the devils Beelzebub and Typhon-Set and had then, simultaneously shaking the peas in a large sieve, called upon these dark gods to confound the rebels with quarrels and discord. This seems to have been one of the most successful curses ever recorded, for having got rid of Mathers the members of the Golden Dawn spent the next few years quarrelling violently with one another.

The Order fragmented into factions, legitimate or illegitimate descendants of which have survived in one form or another to the present day.

Meanwhile there was nothing more that Crowley could do about the situation. He had abandoned the Abra-Melin Operation to fight for Mathers and he had lost. Scandalous tales had been spread about him and these would damage his reputation ten years hence. Although he had finally fallen in love with an American opera singer and even became engaged to her, she went back to the United States allegedly to divorce her husband—and he never saw her again. It was too late to return to the Abra-Melin work, which should be commenced at Easter. In any case, the urge to travel had once more reasserted itself within him and in June 1900 he sailed for New York, destination Mexico.

2

Crowley's time in Mexico was productive. He fell in love with the country, explored its interior and as a result of recalling his affair with the American prima donna and enjoying an afternoon in bed with a Mexican woman of the slums, wrote the poem *Tannhauser* in one continuous sitting of 67 hours. He had an introduction to Don Jesus Medina, one of the highest chiefs of Scottish rite freemasonry, and Don Jesus was so impressed by Crowley's knowledge that he initiated him into his Lodge, pushed him swiftly through the degrees and admitted him to the thirty-third and last one. However, Crowley's principal concern was with his solitary work at Ceremonial Magic. Having hired a house in Mexico City, he continued with the practice known as 'astral travel' or 'scrying in the spirit vision'; he experimented with acquiring the power of invisibility and claimed some success; he tried the advanced Enochian system; he sought to perfect all he had learned in the Golden Dawn; he devised a Ritual of Self-Initiation; and he decided that his results entitled him to claim the grade of Adeptus Major. If he felt pleased with his progress, this feeling was rudely shattered by the arrival of Oscar Eckenstein.

Crowley's friend and mentor listened to his magical out-pourings and dismissed them as rubbish. He condemned Crowley's inability to control his own thoughts. He said: 'Give up your Magick, with all its romantic fascinations and deceitful delights. Promise to do this for a time and I will teach you how to master your mind.' Eckenstein's method was one of severely disciplined concentration. Crowley had to practise visualizing

35

simple objects and then proceed to moving objects. Beside him, to gauge his progress, he would have a stop-watch, a note-book and a pencil. Every time his mind wandered or he failed to hold the image steady, he had to make a mark denoting a break in concentration. Anyone who has tried this finds it agonizing initially and Crowley was no exception; his diary records his failures and frustrations. Gradually he improved until he was also able to imagine given sounds, scents, tastes and tactile sensations to his own satisfaction and that of Eckenstein. 'Under his careful tuition, I obtained great success,' Crowley wrote. 'There is no doubt that these months of steady scientific work, unspoiled by my romantic fancies, laid the basis of a sound magical and mystic technique.'

All this took place against a background of climbing and exploration. Crowley and Eckenstein ascended Iztaccihuatl from every possible side, the Nevado, Toluca and Popocatapetl, breaking a number of world records and establishing new ones, in particular that for pace uphill at great heights. Both men agreed that the next logical objective would be to climb a mountain higher than any previously conquered by man and to this end they would in due course lead an expedition to the Himalayas.

Crowley now wandered through Texas and California and went on to Hawaii. There he fell in love with a married American woman and recorded their passion in some of the finest poetry of his early period: *Alice: An Adultery.*

> This night – O never dawn shall crest
>   The world of wakening,
> Because my lover has my breast
>   On hers for dawn and spring.
> This night shall never be withdrawn
> Unless my Alice be the dawn.

When Alice returned to her husband, Crowley proceeded to Japan and thence to Ceylon, where he was reunited with Allan Bennett.

The two Adepts conferred regarding the next step to take in

quest of wisdom. Bennett was studying Buddhism and learning the practice of Yoga from a Shaivite guru, Shri Parananda, Solicitor-General of Ceylon; for a time Crowley also learned from the latter. In the Summer of 1901 Crowley and Bennett took a bungalow at Kandy for the specific purpose of devoting themselves to Raja Yoga and once more Bennett acted as Crowley's guru. The mental training Crowley had received from Eckenstein proved invaluable for mastering the one-pointed concentration which is the essence of this Way. The matter will be discussed more fully in Part 3. For the moment suffice it to say that Crowley made rapid progress and attained to the first major trance of Dhyana.

> ... *this consciousness of the Ego and the non-Ego, the seer and the thing seen, the knower and the thing known, is blotted out.*
> There is usually an intense light, an intense sound, and a feeling of such overwhelming bliss that the resources of language have been exhausted again and again in the attempt to describe it.
> *It is an absolute knock-out blow to the mind.* It is so vivid and tremendous that those who experience it are in the gravest danger of losing all sense of proportion.
> *By its light all other events of life are as darkness.*[13]

Bennett had attained not only to Dhyana but to the great trance of Samadhi, yet he concluded that these experiences were themselves obstacles to the realization of ultimate truths and resolved to become a Buddhist monk. By contrast, Crowley found it impossible to proceed further. He had achieved much but his interest in mysticism was exhausted. Intellectually he accepted Buddhism and accompanied Bennett on a pilgrimage to the ruined sacred cities; but he would not become a monk.

Instead, Crowley crossed to India and explored its southern provinces, becoming one of the few Europeans to gain admission to the rock temples of Madura, where he sacrificed a goat to Bhavani. He also took up big game hunting, fell in with a hunter called Edward Thornton and navigated the treacherous Rangoon River with him. Bennett had now taken the Yellow Robe and become Bhikku Ananda Metteya in a Burmese monastery, where Crowley again made contact with him and discussed plans for extending Buddhism to Europe.

There was more big-game hunting in northern India, including the shooting of crocodiles, and all the while Crowley was writing poetry. *The Sword of Song* is probably the most characteristic product of this period. Crowley endeavours to reach truth through reason and Buddhist philosophy but encounters paradox after paradox in trying to express or even to think the inexpressible.

> The metaphysics of these verses
> Is perfectly absurd. My curse is
> No sooner in an iron word
> I formulate my thought than I
> Perceive the same to be absurd.

At this time Crowley also wrote a number of superb essays equating Buddhist and Western scientific thought.

In the Spring of 1902 he joined Oscar Eckenstein in Kashmir for their attempt to climb the world's second highest mountain, K2 or Chogo Ri. The other members of the expedition were H. Pfannl and B. Wessely from Austria, Dr J. Jacot Guillarmod from Switzerland and Guy Knowles, a Cambridge man. They established a camp at twenty-one thousand feet and Crowley reached the height of over twenty-two thousand feet before abominable weather conditions, including an almost interminable blizzard, forced them to turn back. This record would not be surpassed until the 1920s nor would that of having spent 68 days on the Baltoro glacier, but the expedition had nevertheless failed in its main objective and this would colour Crowley's attitude.

In the late Autumn, he arrived in Paris possessed by a mood of harsh scepticism. He felt he had gone around the globe singing 'Nearer my God to Thee' only to return to the beginning and his original Trance of Sorrow back in 1897. Everything seemed pointless. Even mountaineering was just an interesting way of passing the time. The Buddhists were right and Existence is Suffering. The goal is therefore the unenticing one of Non-

Existence or Nirvana; and he would send his friends bitter New Year postcards inscribed: 'Wishing you a speedy termination of Existence.'

Perhaps Mathers could inspire him once more? Crowley's visit did not go well. Mathers displayed no interest at all in the sublimities of Eastern thought. According to Crowley, he had clung to his ego and Adeptship instead of proceeding to annihilate them in a mystic marriage with the Universe, succumbed to the Abra-Melin demons he had unwittingly evoked, lost his honoured place before the Secret Chiefs and degenerated into an unproductive drunkard. Brother Perdurabo was bitterly disillusioned. Magic was true; he had seen and done it for himself; it was a technique which got results just like fishing; and it led absolutely nowhere.

He threw himself into the artistic and bohemian life of Paris. His old friend Gerald Kelly was living there and painting: they had kept in touch by letter while Crowley went around the world. Together they became the lions of the circle which gathered at Le Chat Blanc. Crowley met Marcel Schwob, Arnold Bennett and Somerset Maugham who would make him the villain of his early novel *The Magician*; and he collaborated with Rodin, whom he greatly admired, to produce *Rodin in Rime*, lithographs of sketches accompanied by the poems they inspired.

On returning to Boleskine in 1903, Crowley made a few half-hearted stabs at magical practices. When this failed to satisfy, he went salmon fishing and took up golf, acquiring in time the formidable handicap of four. Without taking the matter too seriously, he adopted the persona of the Highland laird. He had already posed as Aleister MacGregor at Boleskine between 1899 and 1900, but now found this too prosaic and became Lord Boleskine.

There was poetry to be written and published too. Through the agency of Gerald Kelly, *The Mother's Tragedy*, *The Soul of Osiris* and *Tannhauser* had appeared and these were followed by *Ahab*, *The Star and the Garter*, *Alice: An Adultery*, and *The Sword of Song*. Reviews were again mixed. The *St. James Gazette* condemned 'A jumble of cheap profanity, with clever handling of metre and rhyme', but the *Literary Guide* called *The*

Sword of Song 'a masterpiece of learning and satire' and the poet 'one of the most brilliant of contemporary writers'.

Crowley was studying Western Philosophy, hoping to find truth in pure reason, and Cerebral Neurology, to which he was now tempted to reduce the phenomena of Magic. He felt he ought to recommence the Abra-Melin Operation because it was there—and after all it should not be left unfinished. The Holy Guardian Angel might be a figment of his brain but so was everything else he perceived and the Angel might do more for him than golf. It was in this frame of mind that he accepted an invitation from Gerald Kelly to join his party at Strathpeffer.

One member of this party was Kelly's sister Rose, a vivacious and extremely attractive, if sometimes empty-headed, woman. She confided in Crowley that she had a problem. She had been having a satisfactory affair with a married man named Frank Summers but her family insisted that she marry a Mr Howell whom she did not love at all. This aroused Crowley's indignation and he proposed a curious solution. Rose should marry him and then do whatever she wanted, including carrying on as Frank Summers' mistress. Rose agreed and they dashed off to Dingwall and were wed in the Registry Office. Crowley fully expected that this would be the end of the matter but to his astonishment, Rose forgot Mr Frank Summers and fell in love with him. To his even greater astonishment, her love stimulated his. He carried her back to Boleskine and discovered that he was 'married to one of the most beautiful and fascinating women in the world'.

The couple enjoyed 'an uninterrupted sexual debauch'. Crowley wanted 'to adorn the celebration of our love by setting it in a thousand suave and sparkling backgrounds', for 'the love of my wife had made me the richest man on earth.' They journeyed to Paris, Marseilles, Naples and Cairo, where they spent a night in the King's Chamber of the Great Pyramid and Crowley showed off his Magic by illuminating the chamber with astral light. On they went to Ceylon where Crowley took Rose into the jungle for big game hunting. One night in their tent he wrote *Rosa Mundi*, his most exquisite love poem.

Rose of the World!
Red glory of the secret heart of Love:
Red flame, rose-red, most subtly curled
Into its own infinite flower, all flowers above!
Its flower in its own perfumed passion,
Its faint sweet passion, folded and furled
In flower fashion;
And my deep spirit taking its pure part
Of that voluptuous heart
Of hidden happiness!

Crowley's happiness was complete when Rose informed him that she was pregnant. They returned to Cairo where he adopted the guise of Prince Chioa Khan of Persia and it was there in the early spring of 1904 that the event took place which Crowley would regard as the most important of his entire life.

Rose, who had little interest in Magic, asked Crowley to perform a minor ritual purely out of curiosity. Soon afterwards, she was possessed by a strange inspiration and declared to her husband that 'they are waiting for you', eventually informing him that 'they' meant in particular the god Horus. A sceptical Crowley carried out a series of tests based on the traditional correspondences of the god and although Rose had no knowledge at all of occultism, she guessed correctly every time against total odds of 21,168,000 to 1. Some bewildering coincidences followed, all of which identified Crowley with The Beast 666 of *Revelations*. The upshot of all this was that Crowley performed an invocation to Horus and obeyed his wife's instructions to sit at a desk in his hotel room on 8, 9 and 10 April between 12 noon and 1 pm. A being which announced itself as Aiwass appeared behind him on each occasion and dictated to him the three chapters of a book called *Liber AL vel Legis* or *The Book of the Law*.

Judged on one level, *The Book of the Law* is an extraordinarily beautiful prose-poem. But it declares itself to be much, much more. It proclaimed nothing less than that an age had come to an end—that of Osiris, the god who died and rose again and is also known as Adonis, Attis, Dionysus and Jesus Christ; and that the age of Horus, the Crowned and Conquering Child, had replaced

41

it. Crowley was hailed as The Beast 666, Prophet of a New Aeon, in which the supreme commandment would be: *Do what thou wilt shall be the whole of the Law.*

Again, this matter will be set forth in more detail in Part 3. For the present it is merely necessary to note that Crowley rejected the role which had been so unexpectedly thrust upon him and found *The Book of the Law* to be uncomfortable reading. As a philosophical Buddhist, he could not accept its bald assertion that 'Existence is pure joy.' As a Romantic humanitarian, he was put off by its exaltation in the destruction of the old aeon. As a sceptic, he was embarrassed by its hailing of him as The Beast 666, come to destroy the power of Christianity and liberate Mankind, for he regarded credence in oneself as The Great Prophet as evidence of delusion and insanity. Within a short space of time he would lose the manuscript. In later life he would come to see the ensuing five years as a futile fight against an inevitable destiny.

3

Back at Boleskine with a pregnant Rose, Crowley made a few spasmodic attempts at keeping up magical practices. One of the few initial results of receiving *The Book of the Law* had been his letter to Mathers, which informed the latter that Crowley had replaced him as messenger of the Secret Chiefs. Mathers responded with a magical assault which killed Crowley's pack of bloodhounds and made the servants ill—or so Crowley claimed; and he counter-attacked by evoking Beelzebub and his 49 servitors to plague Mathers.

Yet there was little dedicated magical or mystical work. Crowley was occupied with the visits of friends like Dr Percival Bott and a surgeon called Ivor Back, and he entertained them with rock-climbing, poetry and practical jokes. In July Rose gave birth to a daughter they called Nuit Ma Ahathoor Hecate

Sappho Jezebel Lilith and, during his wife's convalescence, Crowley sought to entertain her with the writing of *Snowdrops from a Curate's Garden*. This consisted of a witty parody of pornographic novels accompanied by verses which vary from the amusingly obscene to the scatological. Yet this Edwardian 'happiest house-party in the Highlands' appears to have enjoyed them.

He founded a publishing company, sarcastically named The Society for the Propagation of Religious Truth, and more of his works were printed: *Why Jesus Wept, The Argonauts, Oracles*; the work Crowley himself admitted to be monumentally boring—*Orpheus; Rosa Mundi and other Love Songs, Gargoyles* and, issued in three closely printed volumes in 1905-7, *The Collected Works of Aleister Crowley*. Some reviewers remained hostile, some praised him. Others openly confessed their inability to understand him. But G.K. Chesterton, while criticizing Crowley's varied points of view, nevertheless declared: 'Mr Aleister Crowley has always been, in my opinion, a good poet.'[14]

There was a long and enjoyable Winter Season in St Moritz with Rose, then a return to Boleskine. In April 1905, an old mountaineering friend arrived, Dr Jacot Guillarmod, and Crowley could not resist taking him on an arduous hunt for a wild and ferocious Highland beast called the haggis: Guillarmod duly shot a disguised elderly ram in the fog and was solemnly presented with its horns as a trophy of his prowess. On a more serious note, the Swiss doctor was keen to attack the Himalayas once again and proposed an expedition to conquer the third highest mountain in the world, Kangchenjunga. Oscar Eckenstein was invited. He was still a strong friend and he adored Rose; but he said he would never again climb with Guillarmod and advised Crowley not to do so either. However, Crowley was eager to capture the record of having reached a higher point on any mountain than any other climber—most probably held at that time by an Eckenstein-trained man, Matthias Zurbriggen, on Aconagua—and agreed to join Dr Guillarmod on condition that his instructions as acknowledged leader would be implicitly obeyed.

Two Swiss, A. Pache and C. Reymond, and an Italian hotelkeeper, A.C.R. de Righi, joined the expedition which commenced in the summer of 1905. It started well enough but soon ran into difficulties occasioned by constant quarrelling between Crowley and Guillarmod. Crowley accused the latter of wilfully and senselessly breaking their signed agreement, whereby he was leader, and of stupid and hysterical behaviour which endangered lives. Guillarmod called Crowley a careless and unscrupulous individual. It is difficult to ascertain the truth of the matter but it can certainly be said that whilst Crowley's account is logical and coherent, that of Guillarmod in *Au Kangchenjunga* is riddled with baffling and self-contradictory statements.

Crowley had established Camp 5 at twenty to twenty-one thousand feet when the quarrelling erupted into open mutiny. Guillarmod, Pache and Righi walked out, ignored Crowley's warnings, took with them the seventeen to twenty coolies they had brought up and started their descent to Camp 4. In the course of this they were hit by an avalanche. Pache and three coolies died. Crowley ignored the cries of the mutineers. 'There was, furthermore, no indication as to why they were yelling. They had been yelling all day.' In the morning Crowley descended, attended to the burial of the dead, quarrelled further with Guillarmod about everything from mountains to money and left the expedition in disgust.

His mood was savage: 'After five years of folly and weakness, miscalled politeness, tact, discretion, care for the feelings of others, I am weary of it,' he wrote to Gerald Kelly. 'I say today: to hell with Christianity, Rationalism, Buddhism, all the lumber of the centuries. I bring you a positive and primaeval fact, Magic by name; and with this I will build me a new Heaven and a new Earth. I want none of your faint approval or faint dispraise; I want blasphemy, murder, rape, revolution, anything, bad or good, but strong.'

There was plenty of this, of course, in *The Book of the Law* but he refused to acknowledge the fact. However, he did take up magical practices once again and established regular communication with Elaine Simpson, a former mistress and Golden Dawn member, who was thousands of miles away in England.[15] He studied Sufism and wrote a book of ghazals called the *Bagh-i-*

Muatter. This he described as 'a complete treatise on mysticism, expressed in the symbolism prescribed by Persian piety' though many have seen in it little more than obscene homosexual verses. He wandered through India, writing more poetry and shooting more big game until he reached Calcutta. There he was attacked one night by six natives armed with knives; he pulled out his Webley and killed two of them.

This incident necessitated a speedy departure from Calcutta with Rose, who had just joined him. They sailed to Rangoon and stayed with Allan Bennett who advised Crowley on certain practices of mysticism. Then, in December 1905, he took his wife, child, nanny and coolies on an expedition through Southern China, a country which made a deep and abiding impression upon him. During this journey, he engaged in the most demanding magical work of his career so far.

Philosophically and intellectually, Crowley felt he had come to a dead end. On 19 November 1905 he had written in his Magical Diary:

> I realize in myself the perfect impossibility of reason; suffering great misery. I am as one who should have plumed himself for years upon the speed and strength of a favourite horse, only to find not only that its speed and strength were illusory, but that it was not a real horse at all, but a clothes-horse. There being no way—no conceivable way—out of this awful trouble gives that hideous despair which is only tolerable because in the past it has ever been the Darkness of the Threshold. But this is far worse than ever before; I wish to go from A to B; and I am not only a cripple, but there is no such thing as space. I have to keep an appointment at midnight; and not only is my watch stopped but there is no such thing as time ... But surely I am not a dead man at thirty!

For Crowley, the only way out of this dilemma was a return to the work he had still not completed, the obtaining of the Knowledge and Conversation of his Holy Guardian Angel. True, he did not have a Temple, but the practice of Magic and Mysticism had led to his acquiring powers of visualization and concentration far in excess of the average; he therefore constructed his Temple in his imagination and commenced with what he called 'the Augoeides'. These invocations were performed continuously as he travelled across China. It was excruciatingly arduous work and beset by doubts expressed in *The King-Ghost*, written at the time:

> The King-Ghost boasts eternal usurpature;
> > For in this pool of tears his fingers fret
> I had imagined, by enduring nature,
> > The twin gods 'Thus-will-I' and 'May-be-yet.'
> > God, keep us most from ill,
> > What time the King-Ghost grips the will!

He persisted with his concentrated aspiration during four months of rough travel along the southern borders of China. After a sea voyage to Hong Kong it was agreed that Rose and the baby should return to England via India while Crowley would go back via New York, as he wanted to interest certain people in another attempt on Kangchenjunga. For the second time he circled the globe, though now in the opposite direction, going via Shanghai, Vancouver, Toronto and Niagara before enduring a fruitless stay in New York. He arrived back in England in June 1906 having worked at the Augoeides invocations throughout the journey.

He was greeted by a series of shocks. Out in the East, his daughter had died of typhoid. His wife was drifting into alcoholism. Although Aleister and Rose would produce another daughter, Lola Zaza, it was against the background of her accelerating dipsomania and the slow but progressive deterioration of their marriage—a process made all the more agonizing by their continuing romantic love and domestic incompatibility.

Crowley's bereavement, misery and a series of serious illnesses did not prevent him from pressing on diligently with the Augoeides invocations. In July he went to stay with his old teacher, George Cecil Jones. Jones had become an Exempt Adept and his advice and encouragement assisted Crowley finally to succeed in performing the Operation of the Sacred

Magick of Abra-Melin the Mage in October. In December Jones recognized Crowley as a Master of the Temple, one who has attained to Understanding of the Universe, though Crowley demurred and did not accept this exalted grade until three years later.

An important result of his magical attainment was the 'reception' of The Holy Books, a process which commenced in October 1907.

> The Spirit came upon me and I wrote a number of books in a way which I hardly know how to describe. They were not taken from dictation like *The Book of the Law* nor were they my own composition. I cannot even call them automatic writing. I can only say that I was not wholly conscious at the time of what I was writing. . . .

Liber Liberi vel Lapidis Lazuli opens with the *Prologue of the Unborn.*

1. Into my loneliness comes—
2. The sound of a flute in dim groves that haunt the uttermost hills.
3. Even from the brave river they reach to the edge of the wilderness.
4. And I behold Pan.
5. The snows are eternal above, above—
6. And their perfume smokes upward into the nostrils of the stars.
7. But what have I to do with these?
8. To me only the distant flute, the abiding vision of Pan.
9. On all sides Pan to the eye, to the ear;
10. The perfume of Pan pervading, the taste of him utterly filling my mouth, so that the tongue breaks forth into a weird and monstrous speech.
11. The embrace of him intense on every centre of pain and pleasure.
12. The sixth interior sense aflame with the inmost self of Him.

13. Myself flung down the precipice of being
14. Even to the abyss, annihilation.
15. An end to loneliness, as to all.
16. Pan! Pan! Io Pan! Io Pan!

The twelve Holy Books written between 1907 and 1911 are exceptionally beautiful expressions of mystical and magical truths and proof—if proof were needed—of their author's exalted state of illumination. Those who study them claim they also have the power to inspire heightened states of consciousness in the reader. In the opinion of the late Dr Israel Regardie, they supply incontrovertible evidence that Crowley was indeed 'a God-intoxicated man'.

However, Crowley continued to create in his capacity as an English poet too, refining his technique in the sonnet cycle *Clouds Without Water*, and then writing the five books of *The World's Tragedy* in five consecutive days. His own comments on this work are marked by his customary swashbuckling swankiness, yet many lovers of literature might be tempted to agree that here he summarizes the range of his own matured poetic gifts:

This is beyond all question the high-water mark of my imagination, my metrical fluency, my wealth of expression, and my power of bringing together the most incongruous ideas so as to enrich my matter to the utmost. At the same time, I succeeded in reaching the greatest height of spiritual enthusiasm, human indignation, and demonaic satire. I sound the gamut of every possibility of emotion from innocent faith and enthusiasm to experienced cynicism.

Other writings of this period included *Konx Om Pax*, which contains an enchanting fairy tale based on the Tarot; a witty dramatic skit; an essay expounding Taoist thought; a collection of lyrics; and *Seven Seven Seven*, a dictionary of comparative religion and magical symbolism which enables one to relate all major systems of mystical attainment. Crowley also found time to travel among the desert tribes of Morocco with the Earl of

Tankerville.

In his *Collected Works*, the third and final volume of which appeared in 1907, Crowley had announced an essay competition in the hope of stimulating critical interest in his writings. This now bore fruit in the one and only entry, subsequently published as *The Star in the West*. The author was Captain J.F.C. Fuller of the Oxfordshire Light Infantry. Fuller would become one of the outstanding military strategists of the century, though his ideas would unfortunately be rejected by the British and adopted by the Germans in the form known as *Blitzkrieg*. *The Star in the West* guides the reader through Crowley's early poetry and is especially valuable for its study of his philosophy. But there is far too much overblown rhetoric and gushing appreciation. 'It has taken 100,000,000 years to produce Aleister Crowley,' Fuller wrote. 'The world has indeed laboured and has at last brought forth a man....' Unsurprisingly, Crowley and Fuller became firm friends and along with Jones they worked to restore a genuine magical tradition.

In addition to attaining the high trance of Nirvikalpa Samadhi by the methods of Yoga, Crowley also returned now to the researches into the effects of drugs upon consciousness which he had originally commenced back in 1899 under Allan Bennett's guidance. One result was his essay. 'The Psychology of Hashish', which anticipated—and was unsurpassed by—similar work done by Aldous Huxley in the forties and Dr Timothy Leary in the sixties and after.

Another notable figure now entered Crowley's unusual life. This was Victor Neuburg, a young poet just down from Cambridge. Crowley and Neuburg fell in love in a mildly sadomasochistic liaison which would last until 1914 and it was under Crowley's influence that Neuburg would write his finest poetry, *The Triumph of Pan*. Together the two friends walked across the wilder parts of Spain and went on to travel in Morocco.

This lengthy affair did not deter Crowley from leading a hyperactive heterosexual life as his marriage continued to deteriorate. A number of mystics and religious teachers, particularly those of Christian persuasion, have insisted on celibacy as a necessary condition of spiritual development. Crowley rejected this idea as intellectually fatuous and morally poisonous: he also wanted to demonstrate that success in these matters depends on the capacity of the aspirant and not upon the favour of any divine being. Accordingly, in October 1908 he conducted an interesting experiment in Paris. The object was to attain once more the Knowledge and Conversation of the Holy Guardian Angel through the methods he had learned while also leading the life of a man-about-town. After frustrating initial difficulties, the experiment proved to be successful and the record would be published as *John St. John*. The ecstasy he ultimately enjoyed gave him the inspiration he needed for the two major developments he undertook in the following year.

The first was the external foundation of his magical order, The A∴A∴.[16] Crowley and Jones had formed it two years earlier but so far only Fuller and Neuburg had been actively drawn into its ambit. During the intervening period, a system of self-development and initiation had been created and this will be surveyed in a later part of this work. The existence of the Order was announced to the public with the slogan: 'The Method of Science. The Aim of Religion'; and it was announced in the second new development, *The Equinox*.

Two bulky numbers of this extraordinary periodical were produced at each equinox over the next five years. As Crowley wrote in *The Confessions:*

> *The Equinox* was the first serious attempt to put before the public the facts of occult science... From the moment of its appearance, it imposed its standards of sincerity, scholarship, scientific seriousness and aristocracy of all kinds, from the excellence of its English to the perfection of its printing, upon everyone with ambition to enter this field of literature... It is recognised as the standard publication of its kind, as an encyclopedia without 'equal, son, or companion.' It has been quoted, copied and imitated everywhere.

Initially, these magical activities had nothing whatever to do with *The Book of the Law*, the manuscript of which had been lost. Crowley still felt antagonistic towards the document and hoped that the whole matter was merely a bizarre aberration in his magical career now over and done with. He wanted *The Equinox* to teach a non-sectarian theory of initiation and the A∴A∴ to teach the practices. However, on 28 June 1909 the Chief of the A∴A∴ and Editor of *The Equinox* was thunderstruck by a curious event. He was staying at Boleskine and searching unsuccessfully for some paintings and some skis when, in a hole in the loft, his eyes spotted the missing manuscript of *The Book of the Law*. This wholly unexpected rediscovery hurled him into two days of uninterrupted meditation. The upshot was that he 'reached a very clear conclusion without too much difficulty. The essence of the situation was that the Secret Chiefs meant to hold me to my obligation... I surrendered unconditionally.'

The Book of the Law became the spine of Aleister Crowley's life. Moreover, Jones, Fuller and Neuburg also appear to have accepted it whole-heartedly, and to have seen it as the Word of the Gods. As is so often the case when considering this strange man, Crowley's own words best describe his state of mind at the time: 'Henceforth I must be no more an aspirant, no more an adept, no more aught that I could think of as myself. I was the chosen prophet of the Masters, the instrument fit to interpret their idea and work their will.' From now on he would be ruled by this belief, that it was his True Will to serve the ends of the Secret Chiefs in the evolutionary furthering and liberation of mankind.

4

Acceptance of *The Book of the Law* did not liberate the man from mortal difficulties. Crowley's marriage came to an end and he agreed to manufacture the evidence required for Rose to divorce him. In *Rosa Decidua* he gave full utterance to his personal pain:

.... Pity! pity! pity!
'Tis like the dripping of some stagnant rain
From the housetops of a ruined city
Upon the flagstones. Not one petal clings
Upon the stalk of life or memory. Stain
Not one pale thought with blushes; my soul's dead
As a corpse flung out of the tideway on
The stinking flats of London mud....

Two years later, Rose entered an asylum, suffering from alcoholic dementia, though she re-emerged to marry one Lieutenant-Colonel Gormley. Crowley commented: 'Gormley claimed to have been flagellated by over two thousand women. I rather suspect him of vaingloriousness: it seems a very large number.' His 'Rose of the World' would live on until the twenties.

In order to avoid the unpleasantness of the divorce case, Crowley left England with Victor Neuburg and arrived in Algiers in November 1909. There he felt impelled to walk through the Sahara and investigate a magical system developed in the sixteenth century by Dr John Dee and Edward Kelly. According to this system, there are thirty 'Aethyrs' or 'Aires' or extra dimensions of super-sensible existence, inhabited by 'Angels' or 'praeter-human intelligences'. In Mexico in 1900, Frater Perdurabo had had visions of the Thirtieth and Twenty-Ninth Aethyrs but had found himself unable to progress further. Now a renewed assault was made on all of the Aethyrs in turn, with Crowley as seer and Neuburg as his scribe. The results have been described in a document called *The Vision and The Voice*.

[The visions] brought all systems of magical doctrine into harmonious relation. The symbolism of Asiatic cults; the ideas of the Cabbalists, Jewish and Greek; the arcana of the gnostics; the pagan pantheon, from Mithras to Mars; the mysteries of ancient Egypt; the initiations of Eleusis; Scandinavian saga; Celtic and Druidical ritual; Mexican and Polynesian traditions; the mysticism of Molinos no less than that of Islam, fell into their proper places without the slightest tendency to quarrel. The whole of the past Aeon appeared in perspective and each element thereof surrendered its sovereignty to Horus, the Crowned and Conquering Child, the Lord of the Aeon announced in *The Book of the Law*.

There were difficulties in penetrating the Aethyrs:

So I consecrated myself by reciting this chapter of the Koran:
Qol: hua allahu achad: allahu assamad: lam yalid:
walam yulad: wa lam yakun lahu kufwan achad
a thousand and one times a day during the march, prostrating myself after each repetition.

In the Tenth Aethyr, he had to confront Choronzon, the Demon of Dispersion, who endeavoured—according to the record—to kill Neuburg by tearing out his throat with his teeth.

The essence of Crowley's magical work in the Sahara, insofar as he understood it, is that he was at least initiated into the Grade of Master of the Temple. Briefly, this entails the 'Crossing of the Abyss' whereby the ego is annihilated. The Adept gives up all that he is and all that he has, even his Holy Guardian Angel, and is reborn as 'a Babe of the Abyss' who grows into a Master. Moreover, *The Vision and the Voice* confirmed that *The Book of the Law* was the Truth of the Gods for humanity; and the duty of furthering this Truth was laid upon the new Master.

Crowley's main efforts during the ensuing year were devoted to building up the A∴A∴ and writing the bulk of the contents of *The Equinox*, though Fuller and Neuburg also made significant contributions. His personal life was enlivened by falling in love with Leila Waddell, a beautiful and talented Australian violinist who joined the Order. In an attempt to energize and enthuse the British public with the beauties of the beliefs he proclaimed, Crowley and his associates performed 'The Rites of Eleusis', which aroused mixed reactions. According to one Raymond Radcliffe, a sceptical financial journalist writing in *The Sketch*:

So ended a really beautiful ceremony—beautifully conceived and beautifully carried out. If there is any higher form of artistic expression than great verse and great music, I have yet to learn it. I do not pretend to understand the ritual that runs like a thread of magic through these meetings of the A∴A∴. I do not even know what the A∴A∴. is. But I do know that the whole ceremony was impressive, artistic, and produced in those present such a feeling as Crowley must have had when he wrote:

> So shalt thou conquer Space, and lastly climb
>   The walls of Time;
> And by the golden path the great have trod
>   Reach up to God!

However, according to *The Looking Glass*, edited by a criminal and scoundrel called De Wend Fenton:

> We leave it to our readers... to say whether this is not a blasphemous sect whose proceedings conceivably lend themselves to immorality of the most revolting character. Remember the doctrine which we have endeavoured faintly to outline—remember the long periods of complete darkness—remember the dances and the heavy scented atmosphere, the avowed object of which is to produce what Crowley terms an 'ecstasy'—and then say if it is fitting and right that young girls and married women should be allowed to attend such performances under the guise of a new religion.

De Wend Fenton now endeavoured to blackmail Crowley on pain of further published 'scandalous revelations'. Crowley emulated the Duke of Wellington in telling De Wend Fenton to 'publish and be damned.' An 'exposure' followed which contained the following disgusting libel:

> Two of Crowley's friends and introducers are still associated with him; one, the rascally sham Buddhist monk Allan Bennett; the other a person of the name of George Cecil Jones, who was for some time employed in Basingstoke in metallurgy, but of late has had some sort of small merchant's business in the City. Crowley and Bennett lived together, and there were

54

rumours of unmentionable immoralities which were carried on under their roof. . . .

This could hardly trouble the celibate Allan Bennett, meditating on the Clear Light in a Buddhist monastery thousands of miles away. But it did upset George Cecil Jones. He urged Crowley to sue. Crowley declined. He argued that he was taken seriously by papers of quality and that smutty tabloids were beneath his attention. He disliked the idea of going to court and having to justify his life in terms of the Edwardian middle-class morality he despised. Going to law is expensive and his money was running out; he had had to let Boleskine. So Jones decided to sue and the consequences were disastrous, as Crowley recorded in *The Confessions*:

When the case came to trial, the defendants pleaded that they had not suggested that Mr Jones was a sodomite. They had not, and never had had any intention of suggesting that Mr Jones was a sodomite. Mr Jones explained elaborately and excitedly that he was not a sodomite. The judge, summing up, said that, doubtful as the case might be on some points, one thing at least stood out sun-clear, that Mr Jones was not a sodomite. It was also evident that the expressions which had offended the plaintiff were inoffensive; that nobody had ever suggested that Mr Jones was a sodomite.

The jury then retired. They were dazed by suppressed sexual excitement. . . They thought there was something curious about the evidence. All parties *breathed together* that Mr Jones was not a sodomite. The latin for *breathe together* is conspire. That's what it was—a conspiracy! So they brought in the verdict that the article was a libel and that it was justified!!!—such verdict evidently implying that the defendants had perjured themselves, that the judge was a fool, and that Mr Jones was a sodomite after all!

Jones now insisted once again that Crowley sue De Wend Fenton and Fuller agreed with Jones. When Crowley declined, there was a quarrel and all three men went their separate ways with bitterness. Others decided that like Byron, Crowley was 'mad, bad and dangerous to know' and deserted the A∴A∴. Crowley carried on, supported principally by Leila Waddell, Victor Neuburg and two authors who have left us interesting fictional accounts of this period, Ethel Archer and George Raffalovitch.[17] During 1911 Crowley wrote the principal 'Magical Instructions' for *The Equinox* and more poetry, in addition to visiting the Sahara with Neuburg once again. And despite his genuine love for Leila Waddell—expressed most poignantly in an astonishing sequence of Zen-style paradoxes published in 1913 as *The Book of Lies*—he nevertheless commenced a tempestuous affair with the voluptuous Mary d'Este Sturges, mother of future film director Preston Sturges and companion of Isadora Duncan.

While Aleister and Mary were drinking and making love in a St Moritz hotel, the latter became inspired by a being which announced itself as 'Abuldiz'. This being or spirit or praeter-human intelligence which expressed itself through Mary d'Este Sturges—like Rose, a woman without the slightest interest in occult matters—commanded Crowley to find a villa near Naples which could be recognized by certain unmistakable signs. There he would have to undertake the writing of a book on the essentials of Yoga and Magick for the general reader. Crowley obeyed the command and found the villa via an astonishing series of coincidences. There he wrote *Book Four*. The section on Yoga has yet to be surpassed for sheer clarity of thought and expression on a matter which is all too often obscured by wholly unnecessary technical jargon. The section on Magick is rather more difficult for the novice, though it is appreciated by more advanced students.

After breaking up with Mary—who is portrayed in Crowley's novel *Moonchild*—he returned to London for another bizarre experience. This was at the hands of Theodor Reuss, member of the German Secret Service, occultist and World Head of a fringe Masonic Order called The Ordo Templi Orientis (OTO). Reuss invaded Crowley's flat one night to accuse him of publishing the Order's greatest and most closely guarded magical secret. Crowley protested that he had no idea of what that secret might be. Reuss pointed out a passage written by Crowley: 'It instantly flashed upon me. The entire symbolism not only of Free Masonry but of many other traditions blazed upon my spiritual vision. From that moment the OTO assumed its proper importance in my mind. I understood that I held in my hands the key to the future progress of humanity....'

There will be more to say about the OTO later. What is presently relevant is that it perceived the sexual act as being the holiest religious sacrament and the core of Freemasonry and magical technique. For his part, Crowley discerned its relevance both to his own private beliefs and to passages in *The Book of the Law* which he had hitherto failed to understand. Reuss and Crowley conferred. In consequence, Crowley became Baphomet, Head of the English-speaking branch of the Order and rewrote certain OTO rituals in the light of *The Book of the Law*, with the full consent of Reuss. He also composed a superb essay on the use of sex for the exaltation of consciousness, 'Energised Enthusiasm'.

Baphomet set himself the task of making the OTO a going concern in England. The A.˙.A.˙. was no longer flourishing. Its number had included Nina Hamnet, the artist; Gwendoline Otter, the socialite; the society palmist known as 'Cheiro'; the artist and magician, Austin Spare. Its 88th member was initiated in 1913. But many had left as a result of the scandalous stories spread about its Founder. He now displayed his faith in the OTO by giving Boleskine House to the Order; even though money was becoming an increasingly painful problem in the wake of the exhaustion of his inheritance.

Suddenly Crowley turned theatrical impresario, formed a troupe called 'The Ragged Rag-Time Girls' headed by Leila Waddell, and put them on at the Old Tivoli. 'It was an immediate success and relieved my mind of all preoccupations with worldly affairs.' The company proceeded to Moscow. There Crowley fell in love with a young Hungarian girl, Anny Ringler, and during this six week period wrote some of his finest poems: *Hymn to Pan*, an ecstatic invocation; *The Fun of the Fair*, a witty satire on Russian customs in the manner of Dryden; *The City of God*, a rhapsody of spiritual intoxication; and an anthem later included in the ritual known as The Gnostic Mass, which best summarizes his conception of religion:

Thou who art I, beyond all I am,
Who hast no nature and no name,
Who art, when all but thou are gone,
Thou, centre and secret of the Sun,
Thou, hidden spring of all things known
And unknown, Thou aloof, alone,
Thou, the true fire within the reed
Brooding and breeding, source and seed
Of life, love, liberty and light,
Thou beyond speech and beyond sight,
Thee I invoke, my faint fresh fire
Kindling as mine intents aspire.
Thee I invoke, abiding one,
Thee, centre and secret of the Sun,
And that most holy mystery
Of which the vehicle am I....

He returned via a sea-voyage through the Norwegian fjords and brought out the tenth volume of *The Equinox* 'despite neglect, misunderstanding and treachery', announcing therein that the period of Speech had come to an end. There would now be a period of Silence; and *The Equinox* would not appear for five years. Instead, he researched Sex-Magick. On the first day of 1914, Crowley and Neuburg commenced a series of homosexual magical operations, recording the methods and effects in a document called *The Paris Working*, and the former claimed to have received great magical insight from what was accomplished. On a purely practical level, one objective was to obtain money for Neuburg, who could then donate some of it to Crowley or his Orders. Certainly—whether through Sex Magick or not— Neuburg suddenly rejoiced in a wholly unexpected period of prosperity the like of which he would never enjoy again. For reasons which remain unknown, he chose not to reciprocate the bounty he had received from Crowley. The two men had a vicious quarrel and parted forever.

When the First World War broke out, Crowley was climbing

in the Alps. He hurried back to Britain and offered his services to his country. Although he was willing to risk his life and had done so on many occasions, and although he had had much experience of foreign travel, spoke a number of languages and had also written a staunchly patriotic article, his offer was declined on account of his increasingly unsavoury reputation. Austin Harrison, editor of *The English Review*, had called him 'England's greatest poet', yet no one even wanted to know about his potential for propaganda. A disgusted Crowley packed his bags and set sail for America in December 1914.

His assets consisted of Boleskine House, which he had donated the OTO; a library of beautifully produced books, written by himself and printed and bound under his instructions—which a wealthy American bibliophile had expressed interest in purchasing for three to four thousand dollars; letters of introduction to useful and influential figures; his magical attainments; a burning sense of mission to transplant the Word to the New World; and fifty pounds in his pocket.

He fully expected honour, success and acclaim. He received, in his own words, 'poverty and humiliation'.

5

Crowley's American period opened with a series of disappointments. Though he was initially warmly welcomed, all promises failed repeatedly to materialize and he found himself unable to make his way into public prominence. He could barely sell one essay, story or poem. The few speeches he made at clubs and societies had virtually no effect. The American bibliophile changed his mind and spent just eight hundred dollars. The result was poverty accompanied by depression, and this even adversely affected his sexual charisma. He longed for Leila to join him; but when she finally did, they had nothing in common any more and the relationship ended.

He tried to repair his fallen fortunes by collaborating with the noted American astrologer, Evangeline Adams, in writing a definitive treatise on Astrology. For a time, all went well. Crowley had enough money to enjoy life and some productive work was done. Unfortunately, his partner cheated him and the proposed work never appeared, though the astrological public ultimately benefited. Crowley's essays on General Principles, Astrology and the Tarot, Uranus and Neptune, were finally published in volume form fifty years later:[18] and Evangeline Adams made money and augmented her reputation through a book whose worthwhile aspects consist entirely of plagiarism from Crowley's notes.

The next venture was much more controversial. By chance, Crowley met George Sylvester Viereck, author, poet and pro-German propagandist, and claimed that through Viereck he stumbled upon the headquarters of German propaganda in the United States, directed by Professor Hugo Muensterberg, which published a journal called *The Fatherland*.

The First World War was reaching a critical stage. There was stalemate in the trenches on the Western Front. Great Britain and France would need the aid of the United States if they were to win; and the aim of German propaganda was to keep America neutral. Crowley's subsequent actions are open to a number of interpretations but certain facts cannot be denied. Firstly, Crowley accepted an offer from Viereck and wrote pro-German propaganda regularly for *The Fatherland*. Secondly, his articles were so ludicrous, so tongue-in-cheek, so bitingly sarcastic and so funny to all save his humourless German editors and readers as to be completely counter-productive. What is the true explanation?

In his attempt at a biography, John Symonds called Crowley 'a small-time traitor'. No sane person who reads Crowley's viciously satirical extravaganza *The New Parzival: A Study of Wilhelm II* can possibly entertain that ridiculous notion. It has also been suggested that Crowley was merely being cynical. After all, the pittance he received for his articles did preserve him from starvation; he was able to smuggle some magical writing into *The Fatherland*'s stodgy columns; and he could justify his behaviour to himself by writing in a deliberately absurd manner. There are some reasonable people who held to this point of view and it has a certain plausibility.

Crowley himself claimed that he was a secret agent for British Naval Intelligence and was working to bring about America's entry into the war—something later denied by Admiral Sir Guy Gaunt in a letter to John Symonds (of course Secret Service chiefs usually disavow their agents, especially those with bad reputations). Nevertheless, the late Gerald Yorke, whose integrity has never been impugned, accepted Crowley's account as truthful; and also the latter's claim that one man who knew of his Intelligence work was his friend, the Hon. Everard Feilding. Moreover, Crowley claimed that the US Department of Justice recognized his contribution when America entered the War in 1917 and gave him enough money to settle his affairs (*somebody* certainly did). Furthermore, Crowley was not prosecuted as a traitor when he returned fearlessly to England in 1919, despite the nation's anti-German hysteria. Finally, a card was found in his wallet when he died, dating from just after the outbreak of the Second World War in 1939; and here the Director of Naval Intelligence presents his compliments to Crowley and invites the alleged traitor to come and see him.

The reader is invited to draw his own conclusions.

Nevertheless, Crowley's activities did engender misunderstanding and opprobrium. Luckily, there were some compensations. His love-life improved, owing to an affair with Jeanne Foster, a sensual married woman whom he also called 'Hilarion' and 'The Cat'. Eventually, she went back to her husband and in a diary written six years later, Crowley admitted that her desertion broke his heart for a time. In fact he was no longer as promiscuous as has been alleged, though his age of forty in 1915 might account for that. In a note to *Magick: In Theory and Practice*, he estimated that he had sex on average about 150 times a year between 1912 and 1928. The figure is surprisingly moderate.

In magical terms, the work accomplished would only show its value in years to come. There were numerous experiments with the techniques of Sex Magick—which subject will be explored further in due course—and his diaries and technical manuals written for the OTO have been found by practitioners of this recondite art to be of lasting importance. He also travelled to Vancouver to make contact with an aspirant called Charles Stansfield Jones, not to be confused with George Cecil and no relation. Crowley regarded C.S. Jones as his 'magical son' and expected outstanding work from him.

However, from Crowley's point of view, by far the most important event of his American sojourn was his initiation into the grade of Magus. According to the teachings of the Golden Dawn and the A∴A∴, there are three supreme grades—or states of being—in which abide the Secret Chiefs who allegedly guide human progress: Magister Templi or Master of the Temple, who has annihilated the ego, attained to understanding of the Universe and whose work it is to 'tend his garden of disciples'; Magus, whose work it is to utter a Word which revolutionizes human thought and feeling; and Ipsissimus (which means 'his own very self'), where the man or woman is wholly extinguished by ultimate identification with his or her own Godhead.

Crowley had finally attained the grade of Magister Templi in the Sahara in 1909—though he had been offered it in 1906—and as late as 1923, when he was dictating his autobiography, he felt he could make sense of his American experience only by regarding it as an ordeal—and ordeals always accompany initiation.

Some traditions have it that only seven human beings have ever attained the grade of Magus: Lao Tzu, who brought knowledge of Tao; Tahuti or Thoth or whoever founded the Egyptian system; Krishna, or whoever was responsible for Vedanta in Hinduism; Gautama Buddha; Moses; whichever man in the Mediterranean basin supposedly died and rose again, known variously as Adonis, Attis, Osiris, Jesus Christ and Dionysus; and Mohammed. Crowley proceeded to perform a ritual in which he formally became the eighth Magus and recognized his duty to preach the Word Thelema—which means 'Will'—as in the commandment of *The Book of the Law*, 'The word of the Law is Thelema'. Henceforth he had to accept the role which the Book had prophesied—the Beast 666 come to liberate the human race.

In worldly terms, this did him no good at all. Though he enjoyed a period of peace and solitude in 'magical retirement' in New Hampshire, then travelled to the West Coast and journeyed on via the South, his purse grew poorer as his spirits sank lower. Wherever he went, he was confronted by scenes of misery, corruption, injustice, intolerance, bigotry, prejudice, ignorance and oppression—and by his own impotence to remedy a single instance. When he reached New Orleans in the course of 1916, he sank into the worst despair of his life and tried to abandon his task as hopeless. Later he would write: 'This action is the only one of my life of which I am really ashamed.' But soon enough he recovered, only to return to New York in a condition of pitiable destitution. The kindness of disciples and friends alone saved him from becoming a down-and-out tramp.

The following year witnessed an improvement in his dismal material fortunes. Crowley was made Editor of a vaguely radical magazine, *The International*, and wrote most of the contents himself. This venture was moderately successful and the imminent danger of starvation no longer impeded his creative impulses. He took up painting, which he would pursue until the thirties. Opinions on the quality of his work definitely differ. Most admit that he has some knowledge of draughtsmanship, composition and colour, though many dismiss his work as amateurish and unhealthily obsessional. Few would call him a great painter; many would laugh at the notion of considering him among the ranks of good painters; yet certain discerning critics have of late come to regard Crowley as the only notable English exponent of Expressionism.

He became involved with one Roddie Minor, who seems to have been the kind of practical, commonsensical woman who nevertheless inspires a burst of creative endeavour. He wrote the magical thriller *Moonchild*. During the freezing New York winter of 1917-18, he wrote *Liber Aleph: The Book of Wisdom or Folly* in which he endeavoured to summarize his entire wisdom—or folly—in 208 chapters of a single page, using the intensely concentrated seventeenth-century prose style originally perfected by John Donne. Some perceive it as a masterpiece; some see no merit at all; and some, such as the late Dr Israel

Regardie, criticize it as 'rather stiffly written'.[19]

Roddie Minor proceeded to make contact, in Crowley's opinion, with a praeter-human intelligence called Amalantrah and this resulted in a series of transmissions which the Beast found valuable. Later that year, he retired to Oesopus Island on the Hudson River, where he wrote his 'translation' of the *Tao Teh King*[20] and underwent a series of trances which included visions of his previous incarnations as Eliphas Levi, Cagliostro and others. According to his friend, the writer William Seabrook, he returned to New York visibly glowing with health and vigour.

After breaking up with Roddie Minor, he met Leah Hirsig, one of his greatest loves. In 1919, the so-called *Blue Equinox* was published as Volume III, Number One, ending Volume Two's five years and ten numbers of Silence. Then: 'I cried like Elijah: This is no country for the poet Aleister Crowley, or the adept, To Mega Therion, whose hope to help his fellow men has this one anchor: Truth shall make you free!'—and he returned to England with Leah.[21]

During his absence, his mother had died, leaving him £3000. There was little in Great Britain which could entice him to stay. The nation which had battled so bravely was suffering from postwar pains: promises to the people were shamelessly broken; ex-soldiers were treated abominably; there was a period of hysteria directed against non-conformists and displayed in the non-repeal of licensing laws passed for the duration of the conflict; and in the lunatic anti-drug legislation, which prohibited purely self-regarding actions. The harsh weather brought on severe attacks of an illness from which Crowley had suffered intermittently ever since the Kangchenjunga expedition of 1905: asthma. His Harley Street doctor prescribed a standard remedy of his time: heroin. For Crowley, the results would be unfortunate.

Nor was this his sole misfortune. As Baphomet, Head of the English-speaking OTO, he was entitled to the use of Boleskine House, which he had donated to the Order, and, when in need, to some proportion of the income deriving from the property if let. Yet during the War the Grand Treasurer, one G.M. Cowie, appears—in a manner which has still not been completely explained—to have alienated this valuable asset; small wonder that Crowley described him as 'insane'. Then there were beautifully bound books warehoused with the Chiswick Press. Crowley estimated the value of the stock at twenty thousand pounds, though this figure is probably a gross exaggeration. The events which ensued defy comprehension. The facts seem to be: firstly, that Crowley owed the Chiswick Press a small sum which he claimed to have paid; secondly, that the Chiswick Press refused to release the books; and thirdly, that by the time Crowley realized his predicament in 1920, he no longer had the money necessary for legal action.

Despite these difficulties, Crowley enjoyed a holiday in Fontainebleau with Leah and a woman they had met on the Atlantic crossing, Ninette Shumway, who had two young sons. Then the party moved on to Cefalu, Sicily, where The Beast 666 realized a dream in founding the Abbey of Thelema. This was a primitive but adequate farmhouse 'in the loveliest spot of the entire Mediterranean littoral'. Crowley intended it to serve not just as a home but as a study centre and Temple of the New Aeon of which he was the Prophet; and he settled down to Magick, poetry and painting. He also continued his experiments with drugs, most notably ether, cocaine and heroin, and analyzed the effects in his diaries.

At first everything went well, despite occasional quarrels between Leah and Ninette over who would be sleeping with Crowley. June 1920 saw the arrival of Jane Wolfe, an American actress. She did not go to bed with Crowley nor did he resent the fact. Instead, she set herself to learning Magick: and she would still be devoted to it and to Crowley twenty years later.[22] 1921 opened well. Leah became pregnant, to Crowley's delight as he worked furiously on writings such as *Magick: In Theory and Practice* and his *Commentaries* on *The Book of the Law*. More visitors arrived: C.F. Russell from America; Frank Bennett of Australia; and Mary Butts and Cecil Maitland from England. The Thelemites were popular with the locals.

With the Autumn, there came a bitter tragedy. The daughter born to Leah and Crowley struggled briefly for her life, then died. 'My faculties were utterly paralysed,' Crowley wrote. The Abbey was further assailed by problems. With a growing sense of horror, Crowley realized that he had become addicted to heroin. Every time he endeavoured to cure himself, he was tortured by asthma—and only heroin could relieve the attacks and restore normal breathing. Financial difficulties grew ever more severe. Leah fell seriously ill. Nevertheless, The Beast 666 persisted with his magical labours and proceeded to swear the Supreme Oath of all, of which he could tell no one—the Oath of the Ipsissimus.

In magical terms, this means that the Magus is dissolved in the Godhead, though the process may take some years. It is the death of human individuality. Unsurprisingly, perhaps, the subsequent period was for Crowley one of excruciating pain.

Money was needed urgently, so in 1922 Crowley visited England and persuaded the publishers William Collins to commission a popular novel called *Diary of a Drug Fiend*. In spite of ill-health and heroin addiction, he wrote the work in 27 days. The publishers were satisfied and agreed to commission Crowley's autobiography. *Diary of a Drug Fiend* duly appeared. Although the novel shows all the effects of hasty composition, it is an interesting and readable account of the causes of drug addiction—and it proposes a remedy. It was selling quite well when James Douglas—now deservedly forgotten but feared in his time as 'The Protestant Pope'—denounced it shrilly and hysterically in the *Sunday Express* as 'A Book for Burning'. The quality of James Douglas's intellect and critical faculties may be judged by the facts that he also savaged James Joyce, D.H. Lawrence and Radclyffe Hall. One week later, the *Sunday Express* made Crowley its target with the following headlines: 'COMPLETE EXPOSURE OF "DRUG FIEND" AUTHOR. BLACK RECORD OF ALEISTER CROWLEY. *Preying on the Debased. His Abbey. Profligacy and Vice in Sicily.*' This was a signal for the commencement of the most disgusting campaign of vilification in British literary history.

It would be hard to find more lies per paragraph than in the frequent attacks on Crowley published by the *Sunday Express* and, shortly after, by *John Bull*. Unfortunately, however, William Collins Ltd was frightened into a cowardly submission, withdrew *Diary of a Drug Fiend* after its third thousand and cancelled the agreement on the autobiography.

A further calamity followed. Raoul Loveday, a brilliant young Cambridge graduate who had taken up the study and practice of Magick, accepted Crowley's invitation to visit Cefalu and brought his wife, Betty May, an artist's model with a reputation as a wild bohemian. Crowley perceived immense potential in Loveday. But in February 1923 the latter died. In a particularly revolting piece of criminal libel, the gutter press accused Crowley of murder.

Nor is there any truth at all in the tale related by John Symonds in *The Great Beast* that Loveday died after drinking the blood of a cat slaughtered in a magical ceremony. The source of this scabrous fiction was a drunken Betty May who needed money from hack reporters in search of sensation. Her autobiography, *Tiger Woman*, succinctly states the sober truth. Crowley instructed Loveday and Betty May on no account to drink the local water. On a long walk, Loveday became thirsty and drank from a spring. He then caught enteric fever and despite Crowley's care and nursing—duly recorded by Betty May—he died.

The assaults of the gutter press became yet more vehement and vitriolic. Nor could Crowley sue his assailants—he had no money, as the *Sunday Express* and *John Bull* knew full well. Perhaps his sole consolation at this time was the arrival at the Abbey of Norman Mudd, another Cambridge graduate, who had been Professor of Mathematics at South Africa's Grey University College, Bloemfontein, and whom Crowley initially called his 'guide, philosopher and friend'. Two Oxford men, Pinney and Bosanquet, arrived soon after for a brief stay. 'They were flabbergasted to find us perfectly normal decent people.' But on the morning of their arrival, there was another catastrophe. Italy's dictator, Benito Mussolini, impelled by his detestation of secret societies and alarmed by publicity, expelled Crowley from Italy.

The Beast went on to Tunis where he was joined by Leah. His situation was hardly enviable. As he remarked in his Prelude to *The Confessions*:

From the start my position was precarious. I was practically penniless, I had been betrayed in the most shameless and senseless way by practically everyone with whom I was in business relations, I had no means of access to any of the normal conveniences which are considered essential to people engaged in such tasks. On the top of this there sprang up a sudden whirlwind of wanton treachery and brainless persecution, so imbecile yet so violent as to throw even quite sensible people off their base. I ignored this and carried on, but almost immediately both I and one of my principal assistants were stricken down with lingering illness. I carried on. My assistant died. I carried on. His death was the signal for a fresh outburst of venomous falsehoods. I carried on. The agitation resulted in my being exiled from Italy; though no accusation of any kind was or could be, alleged against me. That meant that I was torn away from even the most elementary conveniences for writing this book. I carried on. At the moment of writing this paragraph everything in connection with the book is entirely in the air. I am carrying on.

He finished *The Confessions* even though he did not have a publisher, then left Tunisia for the South of France and dealings with that extraordinary rogue and writer, Frank Harris, whom he had known since the days of Edwardian literary London. The *Paris Evening Telegram* was up for sale. Harris proposed that he and Crowley buy the paper and act as joint editors. Each convinced the other of his ability to raise half the necessary cash. Each believed that the other would do so, and once that had happened, the rest would be easy. Naturally, nothing came of this ingenious plan.

Crowley staggered on to Paris, seemingly bereft of all but his sense of humour. As he had recently written about the events of his life in a poem called 'Lenin's Week',

> Monday, I'm murdered: Tuesday I am booked
> For a paralytic stroke: I die again
> On Wednesday from my wounds: go insane
> On Thursday: Friday? ah! my food is cooked
> With Arsenic: On Saturday, Veflucht!

I marry: Sunday softening of the brain.
The week will not be wasted; yet I fain
Fancy there's something I have overlooked.
What is the name of Marx? Have I to speak
Somewhere? or shoot myself? No, that's next week.
I'll have to ask my wife—aha! that unlocks
My memory—where's my note book, I must write
It down at once, or otherwise I might
Forget to ask her please to mend my socks.

Yet his diary at this time is very painful reading. He pawned his few remaining valuables, stumbled to a rented room, lay down on the bed and stared sightlessly at the ceiling as visions of ice and fire possessed his benumbed brain. As Perdurabo, he had sworn to endure unto the End. Now the Supreme Ordeal reached its climax and he could write only: 'I died.'

6

It is said by Magicians and Mystics that on attaining the ultimate grade of Ipsissimus, the vital star which animates a human being is at one with Godhead: yet it manifests itself as an ordinary man or woman with ordinary virtues and vices.

That is one way of regarding the matter. There are others. Some hold that Crowley failed to annihilate a portion of his ego when he crossed the Abyss in 1909 and that this became swollen out of all measure—to poison and ruin him.[23] Many others believe that he was merely a self-deluded madman, compensating for his failure in the world with fantasies of expanding egotistical megalomania.

Whatever the true explanation, Crowley's subsequent actions are hard to understand. There were still the faithful disciples willing to give their all for him and who now arrived in Paris: Leah Hirsig and Norman Mudd. Yet Crowley had tired of Mudd, whom he found pitiful and pathetic; and he cast aside Leah, who wrote in her diary that it was 'damn hard' to think of 'the rottonest kind of creature' as a Word.[24] Instead he commenced an affair with a moneyed American woman, Dorothy Olsen, returned to Tunisia with her, recovered his health, energy and spirits and launched a campaign to promote himself as the World Teacher.

In 1925, one Herr Traenker invited him to Thuringia, Germany, for an international conference of the OTO. Theodor Reuss had died. Crowley was elected his successor and World Head of the Order. There was another benefit springing from his visit to Germany. He discovered a German medical preparation which relieved his asthma and, with its aid, he was able finally to conquer his addiction to heroin. At last he had mastered the drug and no longer had any need of it.

During the next two years, he lived up to the name he had given himself decades earlier—the Wanderer of the Waste—dividing his time between France, Germany and North Africa as mistresses came and went. When the young Israel Regardie sailed from America to become his secretary in 1928, Crowley was living comfortably in a Paris apartment. Naturally the Beast had a mistress; and two other interesting disciples: Karl J. Germer, a Prussian ex-Army officer; and Gerald Yorke, an English country gentleman, educated at Eton and Cambridge. When the mistress or Scarlet Woman[25] left in a huff, she was soon replaced by Maria Teresa de Miramar, a High Priestess of Voodoo from Nicaragua. During 1929, Crowley saw his classic *Magick: In Theory and Practice* through the press and it would be published in Paris and London. But he was also expelled from France.

The reason for this has been clearly stated in *Seven Friends* by Louis Wilkinson, novelist and Shakespearean scholar:

... he was offered a substantial sum of money to cast horoscopes for a girl and a man with indications that the two were exceptionally well suited to each other and destined to a happy marriage. This was suggested by a *sale individu* who would have had a considerable commission if the marriage had happened: the girl was rich. Crowley, at that time particularly hard up, refused. The individual then told him that he could and would prevent the renewal of his visa if he did not cast the horoscope. Crowley, knowing that this was so, knowing the man's back-stairs pull with the authorities concerned, still refused, with the result that he had in due course to leave Paris under the obloquy of having been kicked out.

By this time the Beast was sufficiently notorious for his departure to be blazoned in the headlines of the international press. On his arrival in England, Colonel Carter of Scotland Yard was anxious enough to visit Gerald Yorke and warn him against Crowley. Yorke responded by setting up a dinner where Carter met Crowley: and the cordiality engendered by the occasion led to Crowley's part-time employment as an agent for the department now known as Special Branch. It was probably this connection which enabled Crowley to pull strings which enabled Israel Regardie to gain admittance to Britain—for he had been refused entry.

So had Maria de Miramar and here Crowley's connections did not work. He overcame the problem by meeting and marrying her in Germany—Regardie later called Maria 'a magnificent animal of a woman'[26]—and took her back to England. For a time they rented a house at Knockholt in Kent and Crowley attended to a new venture, The Mandrake Press. This publishing firm issued *Moonchild; The Stratagem and Other Stories; The Legend of Aleister Crowley* by P.R. Stephensen—a well-intentioned attempt to whitewash the Beast—and the first two volumes of *The Confessions*, before collapsing. The collapse was due to both the hostility to Crowley's works displayed by booksellers and wholesale distributors and to Crowley's own business incompetence.

The Wanderer of the Waste continued to wander between 1930 and 1934, particularly after the break-up of his marriage of convenience to Maria. There were more visits to Germany, where one disciple, Martha Kuentzel, claimed that Hitler's rise to power owed itself to her tutelage and his reading of *The Book of the Law*. Crowley also became friends with one of Portugal's greatest poets, Fernando de Pessoa, and visited him in the company of a new Scarlet Woman, Hanni Jaeger.

Back in England, he entered a period of litigation. Given his earlier reluctance to go to court, this was strange behaviour. Perhaps his judgement was awry. Perhaps he hoped to make money. Perhaps he was impelled by a need to keep a legend of infamy alive so as to attract the attention of those with magical potential. His motives are not easy to discern. In any event, he sued a bookseller for libel and won; then he made what appears to have been a serious error of judgement. His old friend, the artist Nina Hamnett, published an autobiography, *Laughing Torso*. One paragraph repeated absurd rumours of the Cefalu period and these were mild by comparison with the lies of the *Sunday Express* and *John Bull*. Nevertheless, Crowley sued the publishers, Constable & Co. Possibly the most notable moment of a most curious trial was the following exchange:

> *Counsel:* Did you not call yourself The Beast 666?
> *Crowley:* 'The Beast 666' means merely 'sunlight'. You may call me 'Little Sunshine'.

However, under the auspices of Mr Justice Swift—a judge Crowley later called 'a notorious drunkard'—the proceedings soon turned into the trial of one who had outraged bourgeois notions of morality. The judge halted the trial to condemn Crowley and invited the jury to reach a verdict to which they rushed with no hesitation. Crowley lost the case.

Another case followed, this time over a criminal matter, in which Crowley was accused of receiving stolen letters in connection with *Crowley v. Constable & Co.*, found guilty and let off lightly. Newspapers rejoiced in slinging more mud in dismal rehashes of tired old fabrications. Yet this kept Crowley's name before the public. Next, the Beast's creditors hauled him into court again in 1935 and made him bankrupt. His consolation was a woman who had witnessed the *Crowley v. Constable* trial and called the verdict 'the wickedest thing since the Crucifixion'. She had approached Crowley in the street immediately afterwards and asked to be the mother of his child, causing him to cry for the first time in years. Yet he duly obliged her request and a son, Aleister Ataturk, was born.

Crowley kept moving during the years 1936-9. He paid a number of visits to Nazi Germany. There is no evidence to support Symonds' contention that he was trodden into the gutter by Stormtroopers (one can dismiss this tale as a wish-fulfilment fantasy) and there was a successful exhibition of his paintings in Berlin, where he encountered Aldous Huxley. Given Huxley's influential essays on the effects of mescaline, published as *The Doors of Perception* and *Heaven and Hell*, one would like to know if it was indeed Crowley who introduced him to the drug, as has been claimed. Certainly Crowley had introduced mescaline to Europe in its smokeable form of anhalenium back in Edwardian days, and he had had much experience of its psychedelic effects; but documentary evidence is missing. To my knowledge there exist just three communications from Huxley to Crowley—and each one consists of an excuse for not seeing him on the date agreed.

Crowley's life in England at this time was busy, despite frequent bouts of ill health. Various vicissitudes of fortune dictated frequent changes of address: Bloomsbury, Paddington Green, Jermyn Street and Richmond, among others. He tried a variety of money-making schemes, among them the 'Elixir of Life Pills' and 'Amrita: A course of Rejuvenation'. He enjoyed social intercourse with a wide variety of people who proclaimed their interest in Magick and Thelema: Tom Driberg, later a prominent Labour MP; Arthur Calder-Marshall, later a journalist and television comic; Montague Summers, scholar; Dennis Wheatley, the thriller writer; Madame de Montalban, witch; Gerald Yorke, who no longer recognized Crowley as the Prophet of a New Aeon but remained a loyal friend; Charles Richard Cammell, poet and man-of-letters; and Louis Wilkinson, who had no occult interests at all but who delighted in Crowley's company. Wilkinson was also impressed by Crowley's culinary skills and after one particularly good dinner when he had been given a book of the latter's poetry, he wrote a letter of thanks which praised the meal extravagantly but omitted all mention of the poetry. Crowley responded with:

On Crowley the immortals ironically look.
He sought fame as a poet and found it as a cook.

In 1937 Crowley issued a magnificently produced work, *The Equinox of the Gods*. This was a definitive text of *The Book of the Law* with an account of its reception. Poor Charles Richard Cammell was so upset by the contents that he threw the book in the fire. Even so, Cammell served as chairman at Crowley's *Eight Lectures on Yoga* and these masterpieces of clarity and wisdom were published in 1939.

War was imminent and Crowley had foreseen it. By this time he had lost all patience with the stupid, brutish and banal totalitarianism of the Third Reich and was telling Martha Kuentzel that Britain 'would knock Hitler for six'. The Nazis had banned the OTO and Karl Germer had spent some time in concentration camp. As previously related, on the outbreak of the War Crowley was invited to see the Director of British Naval Intelligence. We do not know what transpired at that meeting, yet Crowley claimed that he advocated the use of two magical signs which were to boost British morale and were frequently used by Winston Churchill: the 'V' sign which, in magical terms, is the counter to the Swastika; and the 'Thumbs Up', the Sign of the Phallus and Victory, which was published in a pamphlet of Crowley poetry during the most desperate days of 1940 and whose use spread throughout the nation.[27]

During the war, Crowley stayed at a variety of South Coast lodgings and hotels. His health was poor and he suffered from frequent attacks of asthma. Because he could no longer obtain his German medication, he had to return to heroin, which was duly prescribed for his ailment by his doctor; and he again became addicted. However, this did not prevent him from completing a major task which occupied years: *The Book of Thoth*. Working with Lady Frieda Harris as his Artist Executant, he redesigned the 78 cards of the Tarot, which she drew and painted, and he wrote the accompanying text. Most find the Crowley-Harris Tarot to be the most beautiful version extant and many students of these matters hold that Crowley's book is easily the finest and most lucid exposition of that complex system.

In 1945 Crowley moved to his last place of residence, 'Netherwood' in Hastings. This has usually been described as a boarding-house and so one pictures some grim little bed-sit in dismal sea-side lodgings. In fact, 'Netherwood' was a country estate standing in four acres of grounds: death duties had compelled its owner to turn it into a residential hotel. Crowley was comfortable here and the money sent to him by American disciples enabled him to enjoy occasional luxuries like caviar and Napoleon brandy. Recurring bouts of asthma and frustration with his heroin addiction did bring on depression and fits of rage which he faithfully recorded in his diaries. And there were periods of boredom. But there was also a stream of visitors, including Yorke, Wilkinson, Lady Harris, Grady McMurtry, Kenneth Grant and John Symonds.

Symonds witnessed one of Crowley's last recorded flashes of characteristic wit. The two men were in the grounds of Netherwood when Symonds asked Crowley if he had ever seen a supernatural being. Crowley pondered the matter long and hard, as though it were the most profound and difficult question he had ever been asked. Finally he replied: 'I saw a dryad once, peeping at me from behind a tree.'[28]

His work during this last phase consisted mainly of writing letters which answered the questions of a woman disciple and these answers were published years later as *Magick Without Tears*. The clarity of his thought and the rigour of his logic give the lie to all who have perceived him as a raving junkie.

On 1 December 1947 Aleister Crowley died. The cause was cardiac arrest associated with bronchial trouble. Oddly enough, there are three versions of the circumstances surrounding the death. The version given in *The Great Beast* by Symonds is that he died with tears streaming down his cheeks and that his last words were: 'I am perplexed.' The version related to me by Ms Pat Reed,[29] which reached her from a woman who claimed to have been present, reminds one of the death of Gautama Buddha as related by a devoted disciple: for Crowley is alleged to have passed from Samadhi to Super-Samadhi to Nirvana to Super-Nirvana, expiring in the boundless bliss of the Infinite.

The version which I believe to be accurate was told me by the Manager of Netherwood at that time. This gentleman, whom I shall call Mr W.H., also showed me what is probably Crowley's last signature—on the back of a laundry bill. One cannot discern any motive for lying in Mr W.H. He has never taken the slightest interest in occultism; he now earns his living as a chartered accountant; and when we met in the mid-seventies he was astounded to learn that Crowley had made a come-back and kept saying: 'Well, I never.' According to Mr W.H., Crowley used to pace up and down his living-room. One day the Beast was pacing and Mr W.H. was on the floor below, polishing furniture. Suddenly there was a crash. Mr W.H. went upstairs and entered Crowley's rooms to find him dead on the floor.[30]

On 5 December 1947 'The Last Ritual' took place at Brighton Crematorium, attended by a congregation made up of friends, admirers, disciples and newspaper reporters. As requested by Crowley, Louis Wilkinson read the *Hymn to Pan* and the *Anthem* from the Gnostic Mass, after which the Beast was cremated. Brighton Town Council was scandalized by these dignified proceedings and resolved that nothing like them would ever be allowed to happen on Council property again.

Crowley's will was proved at eighteen pounds.

Confusion surrounds the fate of Crowley's ashes. As he requested, these were placed in an urn and given to his successor as World Head of the OTO, Karl J. Germer. According to one account, the urn was stolen from Germer's home and its whereabouts are unknown. According to another, Germer buried the urn by a tree in his garden but when he moved house, even though he dug all the way round the roots of the tree, he could not find it.

As Crowley wrote in *Konx Om Pax*:

> Bury me in a nameless grave!
> I came from God the world to save.
> I brought them wisdom from above:
> Worship, liberty and love.
> They slew me for I did disparage
> Therefore Religion, Law and Marriage.

So be my grave without a name
That earth may swallow up my shame!

Poor, obscure, ridiculed, hated and dismissed as an evil lunatic and failure, the Great Beast was finally dead and gone. Yet future generations would cry: 'The Beast is dead. Long live the Beast!'

Notes

1. Israel Regardie's *The Eye in the Triangle* is the finest study of Crowley; *The Beast*, by Dan Mannix, the silliest.

2. See Part Five.

3. Yorke swore an oath during his time as a Crowley disciple that he would preserve all documents given to him by Crowley, and he adhered to this oath even after he repudiated Crowley as a Prophet and Guru. Throughout his life Yorke continued to collect Crowley material.

4. In a letter to his son of 30 May 1947, Aleister Ataturk, conceived with Patricia MacAlpine, Crowley states: 'One of your Ancestors was Duke of a place called La Querouaille in Brittany, and he came over to England with the Duke of Richmond... Owing to the French Revolution and various other catastrophes, the Dukedom is no longer in existence legally....'

5. Gerald Yorke's opinion, recalling Crowley's reminiscences, in private conversation with the author.

6. Louis Marlow (pseudonym of Louis Wilkinson), *Seven Friends*.

7. In *The Confessions* Crowley states: 'There is a great deal more to this story; but I may not tell it—yet.' I have been unable to discover the truth here.

8. T.G. Longstaff, *This My Voyage*.

9. The controversy can be studied in Ellic Howe's *The Magicians of the Golden Dawn* (London 1972), in which it is skilfully argued that the Order was founded on a fraud, and my own 'Suster's Answer to Howe' (in Regardie's *What You Should Know About the Golden Dawn*, Phoenix 1983) which raises questions Howe has failed to consider and reaches a verdict of 'Not Proven'.

A third possibility—which should be given serious consideration—has since been suggested in private conversation by Eric Towers and others: that Westcott was a forger but that the result was nevertheless enough for Mathers to generate genuine Magic.

In the end, of course, the question of origins is of purely academic interest. Either Golden Dawn magic works or it does not.

10. Introduction to *Aleister Crowley: Selected Poems*, edited by Martin Booth (Crucible 1986).

11. See Bax, *Some I Knew Well* and *Inland Far*.

12. 'We were partially successful; a helmeted head and the left leg being distinctly solid, though the rest of the figure was cloudy and vague. But the operation was in fact a success in the following manner. . . .' Crowley peremptorily demanded £100 from a mistress he was leaving. Surprisingly, she gave it to him, and this money paid for Bennett's passage to Ceylon. See *The Confessions*.

13. Crowley, *Book Four*.

14. *Daily News*, September 1904.

15. This extraordinary tale is related in *The Confessions*.

16. Astrum Argenteum: Silver Star.

17. See Archer, *The Hieroglyph* and Raffalovitch, *The Deuce And All*.

18. See Aleister Crowley, *Astrology,* edited by Stehen Skinner; and Aleister Crowley, *The Complete Astrological Writings*, edited by Symonds and Grant.

19. Letter to the author, 1971.

20. In fact Crowley could not read Chinese. He rewrote the Legge translation in the light of his own mystical experience.

21. To Mega Therion: Great Wild Beast.

22. Her letters, many of which are preserved in the Yorke Collection, reveal a lively and attractive personality, combined with integrity.

23. See Regardie, *The Eye In The Triangle* for an interesting analysis, albeit a controversial one.

24. Certain Magicians argue that the relationship came to an end because all necessary magical work had been done.

25. See Part 3.

26. Private conversation with the author, 1982.

27. In a review of Symonds' *The Great Beast*, Maurice Richardson recalls lunching with Crowley at a club patronized mainly by Naval officers, with whom Crowley appeared to be on friendly and familiar terms.

28. John Symonds, *The Magic of Aleister Crowley*. Symonds took Crowley seriously and so the passage, which ends the book, is (unintentionally) doubly hilarious.

29. Ms Reed is the former manageress of The Equinox Bookshop, now, alas, no longer in business.

30. Herr Ralph Tegtmeier, author and translator and Chief of the German Saturn-Gnosis Lodge of the OTO—a section which honours Crowley but which did not recognize him as Prophet of the New Aeon and World Teacher—told me the following wonderful story, a fourth version of the death of Crowley. He heard it from a Hastings bookseller who claims that when he saw a magical sign apparently drawn by Crowley on the external brickwork of Netherwood, he found it so disturbing that he wiped it away with a dish-cloth—and the next day Crowley died. I concur with the comment of Herr Tegtmeier, a gentleman with a delightful sense of humour: now we know the truth at last; the Great Beast was rubbed out by a dish-cloth.

PART TWO

The Legend and the Man

When a man of genius appears, you may know him by this Sign: that all the dunces are united in a confederacy against him.

Jonathan Swift

In 1907, Florence Farr Emery wrote the following in *The New Age*:

It is a hydra-headed monster, this London Opinion, but we should not be surprised at all to see an almost unparalleled event, namely, every one of those hydra-heads moving with a single purpose, and that the denunciation of Mr Aleister Crowley and all his works.

Now this would be a remarkable achievement for a young gentleman who only left Cambridge quite a few years ago. It requires a certain amount of serious purpose to stir Public Opinion into active opposition, and the only question is, has Mr Crowley a serious purpose?... A final judgement is that the young man is a remarkable product of an unremarkable age... His power of expression is extraordinary; his kite flies, but he never fails to jerk it back to earth with some touch of ridicule or bathos which makes it still an open question whether he will excite that life-giving animosity on the part of Public Opinion which is only accorded to the most dangerous thinkers.

This 'life-giving animosity' can best be demonstrated via a series of quotations from various publications:

Mr Aleister Crowley's Blasphemous and Prurient Propaganda.

John Bull, 5 November 1910

Whenever he needs money, and cannot get it from fresh victims, he sends them on the streets of Palermo or Naples to earn it for him. He served once a prison sentence in America for procuring young girls for a similar purpose.

Sunday Express, 26 November 1922

A large number of his books are printed privately—some of them in Paris. They are either incomprehensible or disgusting— generally both. His language is the language of a pervert and his ideas are negligible.

Sunday Express, 26 November 1922

NEW SINISTER REVELATIONS OF ALEISTER CROWLEY VARSITY LAD'S DEATH ENTICED TO 'ABBEY'
Dreadful Ordeal of a Young Wife
Worse Horrors Still
Turned Out
The Beast's Hope

Sunday Express, 25 February 1923

YOUNG WIFE'S STORY OF ALEISTER CROWLEY'S ABBEY SCENES OF HORROR DRUGS, MAGIC AND VILE PRACTICES
Girl's Ordeal
Saved by the Consul

Sunday Express, 4 March 1923

The headlines from *John Bull* included:

THE KING OF DEPRAVITY (10 March 1923)

THE WICKEDEST MAN IN THE WORLD (24 March 1923)
KING OF DEPRAVITY ARRIVES (14 April 1923)
WE TRAP THE TEMPTRESS (28 April 1923)
A CANNIBAL AT LARGE (April 1923)
A MAN WE'D LIKE TO HANG (May 1923)
A HUMAN BEAST RETURNS (30 August 1924)

On one solitary mountain-climbing expedition it is actually affirmed that running short of provisions, he killed two of his native carriers, and *cut them up for food!* This incredible piece of cannibalism is cynically authenticated by The Beast himself.

(John Bull, April 1923)

Nor were the American tabloids any more accurate:

DRIVEN TO SUICIDE BY DEVIL WORSHIPPERS
Wicked Exploits of 'The Ace of Spades', a Secret Organisation Which Preys Upon Superstitious Women and Blackmails Them or Frightens Them to Death by Making Them Believe That Satan Owns Them

SECRETS BEHIND THE SCENES AMONG THE
DEVIL-WORSHIPPERS
A Young English Bride Who Fled from the Sicilian 'Abbey' of the Vicious New 'Do Whatever You Want' Religion, Reveals the Wicked Rituals Carried On by Its 'High Priest' and His Worshippers.

THE ANGEL CHILD WHO 'SAW HELL' AND CAME
BACK
Heartfelt Confessions of the London Art Model Who Turned Apache and Took To Drugs and How a Genuine Vision Redeemed Her at the Brink.

There is no doubt that Crowley himself was partly to blame for his scandalous reputation. His excesses outraged the world of his time though they would probably not bother anyone today. However, he did not exactly 'veil his vices in virtuous words' and his blatant non-conformity and wild sense of humour aroused the enmity of the mediocre.

Certainly he had his faults and it is impossible to give the man a coat of whitewash. These faults included vanity and conceitedness; a frantic desire for self-advertisement as noted repeatedly by his contemporaries; an unappealing streak of snobbery, which made him particularly cruel to tradesmen—he often lived out Oscar Wilde's maxim: 'The only way in which one can live in the memory of the commercial classes is by not paying one's bills'; and a tendency to quarrel over petty sums and slights, real or imagined. He frequently accused others of stealing from him on the basis of very slender evidence or no evidence at all. He displayed a vicious capacity for vengeance, sometimes descending to the level of racist slurs when attacking Neuburg, Regardie or Krishnamurti, and on occasion spitefully spread malicious falsehoods about those with whom he had quarrelled. His callous behaviour to Leah Hirsig and Norman Mudd is hard to understand or excuse. The same can be said for his occasional attacks on homosexuals and masochists when he himself was bisexual with strong sado-masochistic tendencies.

Other minor faults were merely tedious: his mania for printing everything he wrote without checking its quality, for instance, and what some might see as his later obsession with vexatious litigation.

In *The Eye in the Triangle*, Israel Regardie employed the tools of psychoanalysis in an endeavour to understand Crowley's faults and argued that these stemmed from his inability to overcome his Oedipus complex and recognize his repressed father-hatred. The interested reader is recommended to study Regardie's skilfully argued case and draw his own conclusions.

It is perfectly possible that Crowley's virtues made him even more enemies than his vices. He was a brilliant man of very many talents—some would say a genius—and distinguished by physical and moral courage, honesty, a sense of honour, magnanimity, generosity and humour. According to Regardie, as long as he did not feel under attack, he was a very kind man.

In common with most artists and great men, he despised bourgeois values, which he encapsulated in the image 'a piece of smiling meat on soggy toast'; and he relished the thrill of shocking the middle classes. His one-time friend, Charles Richard Cammell, manfully tried to present Crowley as a true poet and a genuine, if flawed, English gentleman in his memoir, *Aleister Crowley: The Man: The Mage: The Poet.* Appropriately, he quoted Dryden's portrait of Zimri—a satire on the second Duke of Buckingham—from *Absalom and Achitophel:*

> A man so various that he seemed to be
> Not one, but all mankind's epitome.

And:

> So ever-violent or ever-civil
> That every man with him was God or Devil.

Unfortunately, Cammell rather spoiled his own work by declaring that he would like to forget Crowley's Magick altogether, which is like saying of a limousine that one would like to forget its engine. The fact is that Aleister Crowley believed himself to be The Beast 666 which, esoterically, is God, Man and Animal conjoined. So it should not surprise us to find that he exemplified and personified almost all the virtues and all vices of human beings. He was indeed 'all things to all men'; and all too often those who met him and stared into his eyes saw only their own smirking images.

Perhaps this explains the extraordinary tales circulated about him. Some have been related and dismissed earlier; but there are other things which Crowley did not do, or which did not happen to him, yet which are even now believed by those who should know better.

While a Cambridge undergraduate, he was not thrown into the Trinity College fountain for being 'dirty all over', as stated in Symonds' *The Great Beast.* If that had occurred, Crowley would have tirelessly savaged his fellow-undergraduates in print for years instead of consistently praising Cambridge. In any case, it would have been very hard to manhandle one of the world's leading mountaineers.

Crowley did not flee in panic from the Kangchenjunga expedition, as Symonds alleges. He walked down from Camp V the morning after the avalanche, quarrelled with Guillarmod, attended to the burial of the dead and walked on.

He did not hang his wife Rose upside-down in a wardrobe, a rumour repeated by Symonds. For a start, he loved her—and *Rosa Decidua* reveals his agony at the wreck of his marriage. Moreover, a moment's thought will demonstrate the ludicrous impossibility of the allegation. How on earth does one go about hanging up a woman by her heels in a wardrobe? Perhaps we should be told.

Contrary to Symonds' allegation, he did not defecate on drawing-room carpets because he considered his excreta sacred. Had that been the case, no-one would ever have invited him anywhere. As it was, the poverty he frequently endured after 1911 did not prevent him from enjoying a rich and varied social life which included visits to country houses where he was warmly welcomed.

Notwithstanding Symonds' repetition of the rumour, there is no evidence at all that he ever resorted to blackmailing wealthy women. Louis Wilkinson's tale, related earlier, of his contempt for blackmailers even if they could damage him, demonstrates Crowley's attitude.

In an otherwise splendid thriller, *To The Devil—A Daughter*, Dennis Wheatley relates a story to the effect that Crowley invoked Pan in Paris during the 1920s with unfortunate results: he was found gibbering in a corner; he had to spend six months in a lunatic asylum; and he lost all his magical powers. I wrote to Wheatley asking for his source. His letter of 3 November 1969 states:

In reply to your letter of the 30th, the two stories about Alastair [sic] Crowley were told to me by one of his disciples who later became a most distinguished Labour MP but naturally I cannot give you his name.

This gentleman told me that he was personally present at the affair which took place in Paris.

Wheatley is obviously referring to the late Tom Driberg, the only man who knew Crowley and later became a prominent Labour MP. Yet although Driberg's autobiography relates a number of anecdotes about Crowley, there is no mention at all of this extraordinary escapade. Nor is there any mention of it in Crowley's diaries. And of course Crowley invoked Pan without mishap throughout his life. Moreover, Driberg had not yet met Crowley at the time of the alleged incident. The most accurate verdict is surely that of the late Dr Israel Regardie, who responded to my enquiry with the following letter of 8 November 1971: 'I think Dennis Wheatley is nuts! That is not good psychology, philosophy nor anything else but expresses what I feel about his brand of nonsense.'

The opinions of some commentators are distinguished by a delightful fatuity. Colin Wilson, for instance, in a letter to me of 13 December 1971, perceived Crowley as being sexually inadequate because throughout his life he enjoyed sex with a variety of women—unlike the superior Mr Wilson, who turned mono-gamous around the age of thirty. John Symonds states that Crowley was deficient in imagination because he lacked 'an inhibitory counter-force' and felt compelled to go and do what others merely think of doing: perhaps Mr Symonds would argue that fantasy and masturbation are superior to resolve, practical action and copulation. But connoisseurs of the supremely silly are best advised to turn to the essay written by Oliver Marlow Wilkinson, son of Louis, and published in *Men of Mystery*, edited by Colin Wilson. Here we are informed—among other gems which unite inaccurate facts with atrocious logic—that Crowley once wrote a short story which describes the hanging of a black man by the Ku Klux Klan, following which a KKK pervert slits the victim's belly and inserts his penis. Crowley may well have witnessed or been told of this revolting crime during his travels in the southern United States and so duly recorded its occurrence for the horror of posterity. But O.M. Wilkinson sees this as proof that Crowley either committed that crime or else desperately wanted to commit it. We must therefore condemn Shakespeare for putting out the eyes of Gloucester in *King Lear* or else desperately wanting to put out someone's eyes—and with that, leave the isles of imbecility for the country of common sense.

The legend of infamy persists even today under various guises. What are the charges? One is that Crowley was a Satanist, whatever that may mean. As his writings clearly show, Crowley aspired to union with all that was holy in the Universe. A second charge is that the man was mad, the usual boring accusation hurled against anyone who desires to expand human consciousness. No sane person can read his writings and believe that. A third is that he was merely a Victorian hippy, a debauched dilettante: the lie is given to this by his extraordinary and recorded capacity for self-discipline, dedication and hard work. Debauched dilettantes do not set world mountaineering records, win esteem for their skills at chess, write dozens of books, master the most excruciating mental disciplines, or persist in chosen course despite difficulties which would make the strongest of men despair. A fourth accusation is that he was just a fool and failure; here much depends upon his legacy, which will be examined in due course. There is a final charge. Many state that whatever may be said in favour of Crowley, there was nevertheless 'something terribly unpleasant' about him. Are they speaking of him or of themselves as he reflected them? And what precisely is meant by the phrase 'something terribly unpleasant'? One can hardly condescend to argue with those incapable of defining their terms.

Crowley's come-back is certainly a curious phenomenon. He died impoverished, abhorred and execrated, victim of a legend of infamy without parallel. Nearly all were convinced that he would be forgotten. Yet in 1951, no less than three books about him appeared. There was *Aleister Crowley* by C.R. Cammell, which these days arouses varied reactions. Those aged over forty tend to find it a charming, well-written and well-intentioned memoir which is particularly notable for its appreciation of Crowley's poetry. Those under forty tend to condemn it as wimpish. That epithet is surely more applicable to Arthur Calder-Marshall's *The Magic of my Youth*. This autobiographical account is well written and paints an enchanting portrait of Victor Neuburg, but nobody born after 1951 could endure the platitudinous sermonizing on Crowley. The work ends with a childish description of Calder-Marshall's meeting with the Beast in which it is claimed that the latter tried to seduce him with an 'hypnotic' stare—whereupon the account becomes laughably silly. Small wonder that the magic of Mr Marshall's youth vanished altogether.

The third study was *The Great Beast* by John Symonds. Here facts were inaccurate, unsubstantiated rumours were recklessly repeated and the author adopted an attitude of priggish superciliousness. The ignorance and malice displayed in the work led Israel Regardie to deplore Crowley's lack of judgement in his choice of literary executor. However, it can also be argued that an appreciative work would not at that time have found a publisher for the mass market; that a popular account was necessary to keep Crowley's name alive; that Symonds was the only one who might be persuaded to undertake the task if offered the position of literary executor; that *The Great Beast* has indeed kept Crowley's name alive; and that therefore the dying man was not quite as foolish as would initially appear.

During the fifties and early sixties, limited editions of works by Crowley appeared intermittently. One hunted down and bought his books almost as though one were buying hard-core pornography or—a more appropriate analogy—the writings of dissidents in Soviet Russia. The 'psychedelic revolution' of the late sixties saw an explosion of interest in Crowley, signalled by his appearance, in the Summer of 1967, on the 'People We Like' cover of the Beatles' album, *Sergeant Pepper's Lonely Heart's Club Band*. One by one, his works were republished—and then reprinted.

During the dismal mid-seventies there was a lull. It seemed for a time that the magical revival was merely a passing fad and that Crowley would go the way of bombed-out ex-hippies. But possibly to the surprise of those who did not understand the phenomenon, punk rock brought with it another wave of magical enthusiasm and the first sign of this was a poster advertising Eddie and the Hot Rods: it showed The Beast—with Mickey Mouse ears.

We shall be dealing with the Beast's legacy in its proper place. For the present our concern is the following question: what can be said about the man himself that has not been said in print before? This consideration led me to meet two of Crowley's most prominent disciples, Gerald Yorke and Israel Regardie. The two men came from completely different backgrounds. Gerald Yorke was a country gentleman, educated at Eton and Cambridge; he once played county cricket for Gloucestershire; and his brother was the respected novelist, Henry Green. By contrast, Israel Regardie was an East End Jew who emigrated to America with his parents before he had reached his teens, studied Art at College in Philadelphia for a time, then joined Crowley in Paris at an age when he was, by his own account, young, naive and impressionable. As mentioned earlier, Yorke rejected Crowley as a Prophet but remained his friend and the guardian of his papers. Regardie quarrelled bitterly with Crowley in the thirties and wanted nothing further to do with him. However, the injustice of Symonds' account spurred him to a reconsideration and he was subsequently responsible for editing a large number of Crowley's works and writing the outstanding study, *The Eye in the Triangle*. Each man distinguished himself after Crowley's death. Yorke became the Dalai Lama's representative in the West—the Tibetan sages recognized Crowley as a Master—and supervised the publishing of valuable Tibetan magical and mystical material. For his part, Regardie brought together the disciplines of Magic and Psychology in his many excellent books and was responsible for the survival and rebirth of Golden Dawn magical techniques in our own time.

Both men concurred on a matter which disturbed many: Crowley's allegedly 'staring', 'hypnotic', 'mesmeric' and/or 'frightening' eyes. In *The Eye in the Triangle*, Regardie wrote that he found them simply 'small, warm, friendly and alive' and Yorke assented in a pencilled annotation to his copy of the book. Yorke also told me that he would never forget Crowley's delightful smile of welcome. Although they came from wholly different backgrounds, possessed temperaments which had virtually nothing in common, and were alike ending their days in very comfortable circumstances, both men pronounced the same sentence on Crowley to me: 'Everything I am today, I owe to him.'

It was Yorke who gave me an accurate account of the meeting between Crowley and another celebrated magus, G.I. Gurdjieff, for he was the only other person present. There are a number of false versions, one of which Colin Wilson repeated in his elementary introductory work, *The Occult*. According to Yorke, Crowley and Gurdjieff met in Paris for about half an hour and nothing much happened other than a display of mutual male respect: 'They sniffed around one another like dogs, y'know. Sniffed around one another like dogs,' Yorke chuckled.

'When I arrived in Paris,' Regardie told me, 'I had about twelve hundred dollars on me, my entire life savings. Well, suddenly Crowley said: "Got any money on you, Regardie?" and like the young fool I was, I handed it over and he went and spent it on champagne and brandy—always the best for him—and I never saw it again. Except in another sense. When I was stuck in Brussels for months because I couldn't get entry back into England, it was the old man who supported me financially throughout that time, so it all worked out even. Then when I finally arrived in England, he had a few quid so he sent me to his tailor in Jermyn Street, as I recall. "One needs a good suit in England, Regardie," he said. "Have one made and tell them to send me the bill."'

Regardie was a little disturbed by his first dinner with Crowley and his mistress, a Polish woman known as Miroslava. The excellent meal was served with the utmost style and ceremonial formalities. The young Regardie worried over which knife and fork to use for the various courses. Then, as the cognac came round, 'Crowley pounced on Miroslava and they fell down on the floor and started fucking like a pair of animals right there in front of me. Today that wouldn't bother me one jot, but then . . . I was so amazed, I think I just staggered out of the room.'

One evening, Miroslava had dinner with Regardie, told him she had packed her bags and was leaving Crowley that very night and entrusted him with the unpleasant duty of telling Crowley the news. Crowley received it impassively, then made his deadpan reply: 'The Lord hath given. The Lord hath taken away. Blessed be the Name of the Lord.' And that was that.

Miroslava's replacement, Maria Teresa de Miramar, High Priestess of Voodoo, seduced Regardie during their time together in Brussels. The latter was understandably concerned about The Beast's reaction when, inevitably, he would discover the fact. But there was none. In contemporary vernacular, he was totally cool about it.

On a somewhat more cerebral level, both Regardie and Yorke marvelled at Crowley's mastery of chess. Crowley would play against both of them at once; they would sit with their boards before them; and Crowley would sit in an adjacent room, sipping cognac as he held an accurate picture of both boards in his mind—and go on to beat both of them.

Gerald Yorke once enumerated the qualities in a man which he most admired and gave the following verdict on Aleister Crowley: 'I have never before or since met a man who combined all the above qualities—who taught me so much—whom I respected more.'

Small wonder, then, that Crowley has come back and that so many find his ideas worthy of profound study.

PART THREE

The Ideas

1

Ceremonial Magic

It is most unfortunate that the general public is so ill-informed on all matters relating to Ceremonial Magic. Accordingly, it is perhaps best to begin by stating what it is not.

It is not about naked perverts prancing around a bloodstained altar upon which writhes a nude virgin over whom an unfrocked Roman Catholic priest mumbles Mass backwards in semen-stained robes.

It is not about seedy suburbanites performing silly ceremonies so as to perk up their dreary little lives.

It is not about self-styled gurus, who would bore any sane person to the verge of insanity, imposing upon the impressionable with a preposterous pretence to sources of secret information and claiming an omniscience ludicrous to all save the gullible.

It is not about a hoodoo-voodoo, mumbo-jumbo hotch-potch of bizarre terms repugnant to human intelligence. Nor is it about a merciful escape into a dream-world for the weak and wimpish. It must, however, be admitted that the above five activities have all too frequently been carried on under the name of Magic.

What *is* Magic? Aleister Crowley defined it as 'the science and art of causing change to occur in conformity with will'. A later magician, Dion Fortune, qualified this with her definition of it as 'The science and art of causing changes in consciousness to occur in conformity with will', though many practitioners of Magic would be happy with her point of view. The present writer has defined it as 'The science and art of realising the Divine Self by changing the human self', though this has been criticized as merely enunciating the objective of Magic rather than its various processes.

What, then, is Black Magic? This over-used term is unfortunate. One cannot be comfortable with the racist connotations of the terminology. Moreover, we do not speak of black and white art or black and white science—so why black and white magic? One answer might be to point out that Magic is like water: one can use it to drive a hydro-electric power plant, make a cup of tea or boil one's granny; and that therefore Black Magic consists of the use of energies aroused by the practice of Magic to harm other individuals. Another point of view is that enunciated by Crowley in his *Magick: In Theory and Practice:*

> ... the single Supreme Ritual is the attainment of the Knowledge and Conversation of the Holy Guardian Angel. *It is the raising of the complete man in a vertical straight line.* ANY DEVIATION FROM THIS LINE TENDS TO BECOME BLACK MAGIC. ANY OTHER OPERATION IS BLACK MAGIC.

We shall be further inspecting these remarks; for the present it is important that terms used far too loosely in most cases are clearly defined.

Sorcery is the use of energies aroused through Magic for purely practical, material gain.

Witchcraft, as largely practised nowadays, is a religion claiming pagan ancestry which worships the male and female principles of Nature and uses Sorcery to benefit those involved in that worship.

'Satanism' is a word which cannot be defined in one sentence, owing to the hysteria it arouses, but which denotes one or other of the following: (a) perverted Christians who find it delectably naughty to blaspheme their own religion; (b) wealthy degenerates who want salt with their sex and pepper with their perversions but who at least do not take the accompanying mummery seriously; (c) jaded morons in search of some new kick, who have read some Dennis Wheatley novels and/or seen some horror films or *Star* articles and who then vandalize churches or torture animals while bleating about the Devil; (d) self-styled gurus whose magical practices have brought them a limited charisma and whose egotism is fed by the lost and inadequate characters whom they persuade to participate in black magic; (e) Anton Szandor LaVey's San Francisco-based Church of Satan, which equates 'Satan' with Freud's 'libido', uses ritualistic psycho-drama to liberate complexes, preaches an ethics of enlightened self-interest and (predictably) attracts perfectly respectable yaps and yuppies. It should be clear from the foregoing that serious Magicians do not indulge in 'satanism' or 'Devil-worship'.

What leads people to the practice of Magic—or, as Crowley called it when he restored the old Anglo-Saxon spelling, Magick? Usually, it is as a result of a quest for meaning and purpose in life. If there is none, it follows that it makes no difference whether you try to help humanity, shop for groceries or squirt sulphuric acid at maladjusted children: but if life does have a meaning and purpose, then one should endeavour to discover what it is.

Many have tried and a few have discovered truths which have created new civilizations—for example, Lao Tzu, Zoroaster, Gautama Buddha, Moses, Jesus called the Christ, or Moham-med. Others have contributed in less spectacular but nevertheless important ways. These truths have been discovered by a series of practices which alter consciousness and use largely untapped regions of the human brain. Nearly all teachers of these methods insist on solitude, certain rules of health and something usually called 'meditation' or 'prayer', which is the concentration of the mind on a single word, image or thought.

The brain, which gave Man dominion over the planet, is the only hope for the human race; otherwise, stupidity will inevitably lead to extinction. A very small portion of the brain is used by most people. Fortunately, there exist methods for tapping its vast resources. Though these methods could simply be called ways of increasing human intelligence and potential, they are usually done within the context of a belief system and the goal is given a variety of names—for instance, samadhi, satori, enlightenment, liberation, even the Knowledge and Conversation of the Holy Guardian Angel. Some of the methods used have recently acquired intellectual respectability in the West; Yoga, Zen, Sufism, Buddhist meditation. How curious, then, that Magick, which does the same thing, should so often be misunderstood and despised, even though it is the most Western of Ways.

The method of Magick is to attain a total one-pointed concentration on a desired objective by using the natural tendency of the Western mind to turn outward. The wand, cup, sword, disk, incense, robes and geometric designs utilize this natural tendency to be stimulated by sights, sounds, scents, dramatic gesture and emotional exaltation in order to focus the will into a blazing stream of pure energy wholly concentrated upon a single idea.

Magicians have basic PT: exercises to improve relaxation, breathing, visualization and concentration. They use divination —whether by astrology, geomancy, I-Ching or Tarot—to develop intuition and perception. The exercise commonly known as 'astral travel' or 'scrying in the spirit vision' familiarizes the practitioner with other states and orders of being—or, according to another school of thought (for Magicians are not dogmatic), the contents of what Jung termed 'the Collective Unconscious'.

Evocation, or the calling forth of spirits, can be regarded as just that. Or one could see it as a drastic psychoanalytical process, whereby the spirit is a 'complex' and hence trapped energy. What the Magician is doing, therefore, is releasing trapped energy, hallucinating it as a personification and reintegrating it into his psyche. Or finally, one could say that he (or she) is exploring mysterious regions of the brain in order to activate hitherto unused cells.

Invocation, or the bringing down of Gods and Goddesses, can be regarded in at least two ways. Either there are certain invisible but powerful forces of Nature in the Universe, whose existence is unsuspected by physical science, which can inspire us with beauty and truth. Or there are certain archetypes of the Collective Unconscious latent in all of us which, when rightly stimulated, can inspire us with beauty and truth.

These practices of the Magician are performed within a schema of progress, usually based upon the Tree of Life of the Qabalists. The purpose of this model is not to mystify but to clarify and classify supra-rational states of being. It can be regarded as a map of consciousness and its various states.

Magick and its practices were known, studied and practised all over the Mediterranean basin before and during the time of the Roman Empire. The most unfortunate consequence of the Roman Empire's decline and fall was a relapse by the West into barbarism. Fortunately, the civilization of Islam eventually arose and the wick of wisdom not only burned but blazed, and spread into Spain.

That admirable scholar, the late Dame Frances Yates, attributes the origins of Renaissance hermetic philosophy to the work of Ramon Lull of Moorish Spain. The writings of Lull give full credit to his teachers, the Sufis. And according to Yates and other scholars, this wisdom spread to Renaissance figures such as Cornelius Agrippa, Paracelsus and John Dee. This 'Renaissance hermetic or occult philosophy' can be summarized in the following nine propositions:

1. All is a Unity, created and sustained by God through His Laws.

2. These Laws are predicated upon Number.

3. There is an art of combining Hebrew letters and equating them with Number so as to perceive profound truths concerning the nature of God and His dealings with Man.

4. Man is of divine origin. Far from being created out of dust, as in the *Genesis* account, he is in essence a star daemon.

5. As such, he has come from God and must return to Him.

6. It is essential to regenerate the divine essence within Man, and this can be done by the powers of his divine intellect.

7. According to the Qabalah, God manifests Himself by means of ten progressively more dense emanations; and Man, by dedicating his mind to the study of divine wisdom and by refining his whole being and by eventual communion with the angels themselves, may at last enter into the presence of God.

8. An accurate understanding of natural processes, visible and invisible, enables Man to manipulate these processes through the power of his will, intellect and imagination.

9. The Universe is an ordered pattern of correspondences: or as John Dee put it; 'Whatever is in the Universe possesses order,

agreement and similar form with something else.'

According to Yates, with whom the present writer concurs, this 'occult philosophy' was the essence of Renaissance thought and later powered the abortive 'Rosicrucian movement'. To confine the matter to England, it subsequently filtered through a variety of individuals and organisations—for example, Robert Fludd, Elias Ashmole and certain Freemasons. But by the beginning of the nineteenth century, the Scientific Revolution, so essential to human evolution and to which the Renaissance magi had contributed so nobly, had repudiated its ancestors; and its proponents sneered at the wisdom which had originally inspired it. It was seriously said—and still is by those ignorant of quantum physics—that if it cannot be measured, it does not exist. Nevertheless, this tradition of wisdom, now ill-dignified by the buzz word 'cranky', somehow continued.

During the nineteenth century, the magical tradition passed through the hands of Francis Barrett, Frederick Hockley, Kenneth MacKenzie and Sir Edward Bulwer-Lytton; and was influenced by the work of Eliphas Levi in France and the foundation, in 1875, of Madam Blavatsky's Theosophical Society. Various threads were then knitted together in the Hermetic Order of the Golden Dawn, founded in 1887. As previously noted, the creator and synthesizer of the Golden Dawn system was S. L. 'MacGregor' Mathers. It was Mathers who welded together Renaissance occult philosophy—the Qabalah in particular—with certain of its sources, which had come to light by his own time—and his own inspiration. The result was a body of knowledge and a method for practical utilization of that knowledge. The entire system, the first nine volumes of which fill 870 pages in the latest edition, *The Complete Golden Dawn System of Magic*, was then summarized and synthesized in more concentrated form (160 pages) within a refined paradigm deriving directly from the sixteenth-century 'angel-magic' of John Dee and Edward Kelly. The 'Adepts' who had mastered all the earlier knowledge and praxis consequently found themselves confronted by a new learning which incorporated and surpassed the old, providing the aspirant with new maps for the exploration of other dimensions of existence, methods for so doing, and a language for communication with beings encountered thereby.

In spite of schism and much undignified squabbling, the Golden Dawn survived in various forms until the Second World War. Lately, there has been a revival and currently there are active Temples in Los Angeles (2) and San Diego, California; Las Vegas, Nevada; Phoenix, Arizona; and there may be others quietly pursuing their work. Ceremonial Magick as practised today derives essentially from the Golden Dawn synthesis.

The contemporary ceremonial magician uses a variety of techniques to purify and exalt his body, imagination, sexuality, intellect, emotions, perception and moral character so that he is at last fit to give his personality to a deeper individuality. This is also called the obtaining of the Knowledge and Conversation of the Holy Guardian Angel. Once this is done, one knows one's true work in the world.

But it does not end there. The next task after the stage of Adeptship is to perfect the faculties of this deeper individuality— and then sacrifice it in a mystic marriage with the Universe Itself. (Unfortunately, it is exceptionally difficult to avoid romantic language; or to communicate in words what is beyond them, as all mystics agree.) This stage—called the Crossing of the Abyss—annihilates the ego; 'the dew-drop slips into the shining sea,' to use Arnold's phrase; and there arises a Master, one who has attained to Understanding.

A Master of Magick is on a par with a Master of Zen, or Yoga, or Sufism, for all true Ways are ultimately identical. But Magicians argue that Magick, which arose in the West, is therefore better suited to the Western mind than Eastern Ways. They are likewise aware that just as the Sufis, for example, have been vilified by orthodox Muslims and are only now beginning to receive their just recognition, so Magick has been vilified by the enemies of Light and Truth.

Crowley learned the art and science of Ritual Magick from the Golden Dawn. These days, the Golden Dawn system can be regarded as the supreme harmonious synthesis of classical techniques. Its object is to bring the individual to a blazing consciousness of the white light of the divine spirit within. The process of doing this is called Initiation.

Those who practise the Golden Dawn system, or systems deriving from it, believe that honourably intentioned and technically sound magical work on the part of an Order gives its officers the power to arouse this 'white light of the divine spirit' in others through beautiful but complex magical ceremonies. This is done in stages and by degrees.

The Neophyte Ritual is of fundamental importance. An individual joins the Order and his or her magical potential is activated. As Crowley writes in *Magick: In Theory and Practice:*

This formula has for its 'first matter' the ordinary man entirely ignorant of everything and incapable of anything. He is therefore represented as blindfolded and bound. His only aid is his aspiration, represented by the officer who is to lead him into the Temple. Before entering, he must be purified and consecrated. Once within the Temple, he is required to bind himself by an Oath. His aspiration is now formulated as Will. He makes the mystic circumambulation of the Temple... After further purification and consecration, he is allowed for one moment to see the Lord of the West, and gains courage to persist. For the third time he is purified and consecrated, and he sees the Lord of the East, who holds the balance, keeping him in a straight line. In the West he gains energy. In the East he is prevented from dissipating the same. So fortified, he may be received into the order as a neophyte by the three principal officers, thus uniting the Cross with the Triangle. He may then be placed between the pillars of the Temple, to receive the fourth and final consecration. In this position the secrets of the grade are communicated to him, and the last of his fetters is removed. All this is sealed by the sacrament of the Four Elements.

It will be seen that the *effect of this whole ceremony is to endow a thing inert and impotent with balanced motion in a given direction.*

The newly-inducted Neophyte then studies the language and

grammar of Magick and undertakes elementary practices such as meditation. The next stage in this system is the taking of the Four Elemental Grades. The Four Elements of the Ancients—Fire, Water, Air and Earth—are held to correspond with, among many other things, states of human consciousness which need to be aroused and activated. Hence, in the next Grade of Zelator, the initiatory ritual is designed to bring out the energies of Earth in the candidate. What on earth is meant by this phrase, 'the energies of Earth'? Simply, those fundamental characteristics in the human psyche to which we refer when we make a statement like: 'John and Jane are very down to earth.' One effect of the Zelator ritual should be the increase of common sense and animal strength on the part of the initiated aspirant.

More study and practice follow before the Theoricus initiation, the Practicus initiation and the Philosophus initiation, which work on bringing out further elemental energies of humankind: imagination, intellect and emotion. This is in order to maximize all aspects of human potential which are usually repressed by the conscious ego or suppressed by external society, and then to balance them in perfect harmony. It is intended that the Magician will think with his brain, feel with his heart, lust with his guts and stand with his feet firmly on the ground. By contrast, far too many in ordinary life muddle the matter and lust with their brains, endeavour to stand firmly on swirling tides of emotion, think with their guts and allow feelings to dictate where they put their feet. This wastes energy and prevents healthy psychological integration, leading to endless self-destructive internal conflicts.

It is held by Golden Dawn initiates that if the work appropriate to each Grade has been seriously undertaken and the initiatory ceremonies properly performed, then the energized yet balanced aspirant is ready for the next important stage after nine months of meditating on what has gone before, the stage of Adeptus Minor. Here, the candidate undergoes a symbolic death and resurrection, to be reborn as an Adept who has beheld the Godhead. The next task is the mastery of magical technology, some of which includes the arousal and control of magical power or 'Light' or 'the energy of the Spirit' within the Self so as to transfer it to other aspirants during their initiation ceremonies.

The attentive reader may have noticed that there are other ways of regarding this initiatory process. For example, one could accept the hypothesis that the human psyche consists of 'a ladder of selves'—as Colin Wilson and others have suggested—and that each step on this ladder makes one conscious of a deeper self within until one comes to the Self that is the highest. Some would call this 'God within us'—Hindus call it *atman*, which is the same—and Crowley came to call it the True Will.

Another schema involves postulating that magical and mystical progress consists in becoming conscious of, and then stripping away, the various thick veils of falsehood which surround and smother that Spirit or Will which we are.

Under the Golden Dawn system, the sincere Adeptus Minor must study and practise Magick in solitude as well as with Order colleagues. In Part II of *Book Four*, Crowley succinctly describes the tools of the ceremonial Magician:

The Magician works in a *Temple*; the Universe, which is (be it remembered!) conterminous with himself. In this temple a *Circle* is drawn upon the floor for the limitation of his working. This circle is protected by divine names, the influences on which he relies to keep out hostile thoughts. Within the circle stands an *Altar*, the solid basis on which he works, the foundation of all. Upon the Altar are his *Wand, Cup, Sword* and *Pantacle*, to represent his Will, his Understanding, his Reason, and the lower parts of his being, respectively. On the Altar, too, is a phial of *Oil*, surrounded by a *Scourge*, a *Dagger*, and a *Chain*, while above the Altar hangs a *Lamp*. The Magician wears a *Crown*, a single *Robe*, and a *Lamen*, and he bears a *Book* of Conjurations and a *Bell*.

The oil consecrates everything that is touched with it; it is his aspiration; all acts performed in accordance with that are holy. The scourge tortures him; the dagger wounds him; the chain binds him. It is by virtue of these three that his aspiration remains pure, and is able to consecrate all other things. He wears a crown to affirm his lordship, his divinity; a robe to symbolize silence, and a lamen to declare his work. The book

106

of spells or conjurations is his magical record, his Karma. In the East is the *Magick Fire*, in which all burns up at last.

The essential practices of the Magician—divination, evocation and invocation—have been described earlier. Of these, by far the most important is invocation, for this involves calling upon a God and thus the bringing of divine or super-consciousness into human consciousness. An example might make clearer the nature of magical work.

It is a vital part of the Magician's task to invoke and identify with all the Gods and Goddesses. Suppose, for example, that the God in question is Horus, Egyptian God of War, Force and Fire, the equivalent of the Roman Mars and the Greek Ares. The Magician will furnish his Temple—his laboratory or work-place—with corresponding symbols and things which suggest and reinforce the idea of Horus. These correspondences, which appear to reflect the structure of the tendencies of the Western mind, can be consulted in Crowley's *Seven Seven Seven* or later magical works of reference, and derive from Golden Dawn teaching. The enquirer will find that the Number of Horus is 5—and so employ at least one five-pointed star and five candles for illumination; the Element is Fire; the plants sacred to Horus are Oak, Nux Vomica and Nettle; the precious stone sacred to the God is the Ruby; the appropriate weapon or magical instrument with which to gesture is the Sword; the incense is Tobacco and/or the substance known as Dragon's Blood; the Metal is Iron; and the Colour is Red. The Magician procures some if not all of these and arranges the Temple with as much artistry as he can. The place of working and the accompanying paraphernalia must then be purified and consecrated.

There follow what are known as the Lesser Banishing Rituals of the Pentagram and Hexagram, short rituals designed to prevent interference from any influences foreign to the purpose of the operation. The Magician then proceeds with the business of invocation, endeavouring ultimately to identify with the God. There are a number of tried and tested methods but much is left to the practitioner's own ingenium. Crowley states the essence of the matter in *Magick: In Theory and Practice:*

The Magician addresses a direct petition to the Being invoked. But the secret of success in invocation has not hitherto been disclosed. It is an exceedingly simple one. It is of practically no importance whatever that the invocation should be 'right'. There are a thousand different ways of compassing the end proposed, so far as external things are concerned. The whole secret may be summarised in these four words: '*Enflame thyself in praying*'.

The mind must be exalted until it loses consciousness of self. The Magician must be carried forward blindly by a force which, though in him and of him, is by no means that which he in his normal state of consciousness calls I. Just as the poet, the lover, the artist, is carried out of himself in creative frenzy, so must it be for the Magician....

Every Magician must compose his ceremony in such a manner as to produce a dramatic climax. At the moment when the excitement becomes ungovernable, when the whole conscious being of the Magician undergoes a spiritual spasm, at that moment must he utter the supreme adjuration....

Inhibition is no longer possible or even thinkable, and the whole being of the Magician, no minutest atom saying nay, is irresistibly flung forth. In blinding light, amid the roar of ten thousand thunders, the Union of God and man is consummated.

There is little point in debating whether the God thus invoked has objective or subjective existence. Seven words of Crowley's summarise the central point: 'By doing certain things, certain things happen.'

It is appropriate now to consider Crowley's specific contributions to Ceremonial Magick. What did these consist of? How, if at all, did he improve upon the Golden Dawn system? And what were his innovations, if any? His achievements in this area can be set forth as follows:

1. Beyond all doubt, Crowley is the clearest and most authoritative writer on Ritual Magick. *Book 4, MAGICK: In Theory and Practice* and the magical writings from *The Equinox*, subsequently republished as *Gems From The Equinox*, are

unsurpassed, though beginners initially have to struggle with unfamiliar terms.

2. His magical instructions for practical work are the simplest and most succinct. *Liber O vel Manus et Sagittae*, for instance, is only fifteen pages long, yet it gives instructions for elementary study of the Qabalah, Assumption of God forms, Vibration of Divine Names, the Rituals of Pentagram and Hexagram, and their uses in protection and invocation, a method of attaining astral visions and an instruction in a practice called Rising on the Planes. A dedicated student could easily spend a year working on it. Moreover, the preliminary remarks display a refreshing common sense:

2. In this book it is spoken of the Sephiroth, and the Paths, of Spirits and Conjurations; of Gods, Spheres, Planes and many other things which may or may not exist.

It is immaterial whether they exist or not. By doing certain things certain results follow; students are most earnestly warned against attributing objective reality or philosophic validity to any of them.

3. The advantages to be gained from them are chiefly these:

(a) A widening of the horizon of the mind.

(b) An improvement of the control of the mind.

3. Crowley concentrated on the essentials of the Golden Dawn system and attempted to eliminate the inessentials. In the course of doing this, he perceived the disadvantages of group working, which include personality clashes, squabbles and schism; the difficulties a student may suffer in trying to link up with a genuine magical Order; and the advantages of solitude. This led him to deplore, for instance, the Golden Dawn ceremonies of the four Elemental Grades as being merely a long-winded parade of the occult knowledge of Mathers; and to devise the system of self-initiation which we shall be exploring in Chapter 9.

4. As a result of experiences and initiations undergone after he left the Golden Dawn, Crowley composed new rituals of striking beauty and power. These included: *Liber Pyramidos,* a ritual of self-initiation; the Star Ruby and the Star Sapphire, revised

versions of the Pentagram and Hexagram respectively; *Liber Resh*, an invocation of the energies of the Sun; the Mass of the Phoenix and the Gnostic Mass and *Liber Reguli*, all of which were inspired by *The Book of the Law*; and *Liber Samekh*, which was intended by him to supplant the Golden Dawn Adeptus Minor Initiation and which, when rightly used, invokes the Holy Guardian Angel. There were numerous other technical innovations which lie beyond the scope of this book.

5. The crowning synthesis of the Golden Dawn Way is the Enochian System which Mathers and/or his unknown teachers adapted from the work of John Dee and Edward Kelly. Though further research into this system is needed, Crowley explored it much more deeply than anyone before or since and left us the astonishing record in *The Vision and the Voice*.

6. The Golden Dawn system can only take the aspirant as far as the grade of Exempt Adept, though this may well take the most dedicated Magician an entire life-time. Crowley made a vital contribution by teaching methods which enable the Adept to cross the Abyss to Mastership.

Small wonder that another celebrated but rather less notorious twentieth-century magician, Dion Fortune, acknowledged Crowley as her superior but avoided him, according to the late Gerald Yorke. As she wrote to Crowley on 8 January 1942: 'My mentality always has hampered my work, and, I am afraid, always will.'

Yet although Ceremonial Magick was certainly one of Crowley's primary concerns, it was hardly his sole preoccupation.

There was also Yoga.

2

Yoga

Much rubbish has been written and spoken about Yoga. Advantage has been, and still is, taken of Western ignorance. Wholly unnecessary Sanskrit terms are used to befuddle the ill-educated. The West has to endure a plethora of 'Holy Men' whom the East would regard as clowns. There are 'teachers' who have precious little to teach; books from which nothing practical can be learnt; classes which give gullible housewives fatuous fibs as a substitute for truth. And the test of Yoga's truth is really terribly simple. It is the same as the test of truth in any other sphere of human knowledge. In other words, are the facts correct? How can they be tested? And is the logic coherent? Any statement which does not pass these elementary tests is no part of Yoga.

As Crowley stated, 'Yoga' comes from the same etymological root as the Latin 'jugum'—a yoke—and it means 'Union'. Yoga yokes together the perceiver and the thing perceived, the knower and the thing known—and leads to a union between the two. Yogis declare that the experience of this union is so powerful that it transforms one's life.

However, these simple statements were not understood by Aleister Crowley in the 1890s and it is probably best that we investigate the matter further by observing his progress. In Common with Mathers, Allan Bennett and other Golden Dawn members, Crowley was familiar with the teachings of Madam Blavatsky's Theosophical Society, which familiarized Westerners with Eastern ways of regarding the world. Allan Bennett,

111

Crowley's principal teacher here, appears to have been unimpressed with the general run of theosophists. According to Crowley, at a social occasion Bennett became irritated by a theosophist who ridiculed the notion that there could be such a thing as a 'blasting rod'; Bennett's response was to pull out a 'blasting rod' he had made and point it at the theosophist; and the unfortunate theosophist promptly collapsed as if struck dead and remained in a coma for twenty-four hours. Those who have contemplated the subsequent history of theosophy would doubtless wish the same fate for its current exponents.

Crowley's serious study of Eastern thought only commenced upon his arrival in Ceylon and is reflected in his poetry. Initially, he was attracted to Hinduism because it was similar in so many ways to the teachings of the Golden Dawn. He studied *The Upanishads* and *The Bhagavad-Gita*, which he would recommend to students in later life, in addition to other scriptures and practical manuals. As he realized, Hinduism is a synthesis of the various cults of the Indian sub-continent. A Hindu can believe in any God, Goddess or Gods and/or Goddesses whatsoever as long as there is commitment to the caste system. The caste system is a way of ordering social life. It is thought by Hindus that there are four classes of society: in descending order, these are the priestly caste—the Brahmins; the warrior caste; the merchant caste; and the worker caste; below these, there are the 'Untouchables'.

In common with any sensible Westerner, Crowley had little interest in the Hindu caste system. But he was fascinated by the religion. Why are Hindus so tolerant in matters of religious thought? The answer resides in that noble document of the human spirit, *The Upanishads*, and the sages who came afterwards and created the system of thought we know as Vedanta. This was an attempt to make order out of the chaos of the innumerable Indian cults. Vedanta is the supreme expression of the Hindu religion and justifies the superstitious behaviour of the peasants.

The ultimate reality is called Brahman. Brahman is the utterly impersonal force out of which the Universe derives its manifestation. Brahman is neither male nor female. It is beyond manifestation; it is the ultimate reality. Everything that is not Brahman is Maya, or illusion. In other words, the manifested Universe is an illusion. We, as imperfect beings, have to deal with this illusion. There is something within us which knows it is an illusion. This something is called 'atman'—the ultimate spirit or soul—and it is part of Brahman. It is, if one chooses to express it in this way, God within us. According to Vedanta, our aim must be to be one with our atman and so part of Brahman. That, it is declared, is our *raison d'être*.

The attentive reader will no doubt have spotted an obvious objection here. What is the point of not being one with Brahman, and existing in Maya or illusion, only in order ultimately to become one with it? The answer is best left to Hindu theologians. My purpose is simply to expound and explain their viewpoint insofar as it can be done.

It is believed that nearly all sentient beings are not one with Brahman—a proposition with which one can readily concur— and so exist in the world of Maya, or illusion. How does Brahman manifest here?

This is where the Gods come in. It is held that just as Brahman manifests in the form of Matter in the Universe, so does Its Energy manifest in the force of Gods—and Goddesses. The initial manifestation in a Universe of illusion is normally portrayed as a trinity of Gods—Brahma the Creator; Vishnu the Preserver; and Shiva the Destroyer. These three Powers have Goddesses with whom they consort and they manifest more densely as other Gods and Goddesses. These in turn manifest yet more densely, and on every level of human life, the result being roughly 320 million deities, all of whom are part of Brahma, Vishnu or Shiva, and hence part of Brahman. Thus when a peasant chooses to worship the divinity of his fire-place, responsible to the divinity of his village, he is worshipping an aspect of Brahman and thus making contact with It.

In addition, there is the doctrine of *avatars*. This means that a God or Goddess can come to Earth in a human body. The most famous example of this is Krishna, an *avatar* of Vishnu the Preserver, but there are many others. Thus it would be perfectly possible to revere Jesus Christ as an *avatar* of God while remaining a pious Hindu.

Finally, there is the belief in reincarnation. It is held that the atman migrates from body to body over the ages. We die only to be reborn in a future life. The ultimate aim is to attain *moksha* or 'liberation' whereby we become one with Brahman.

Any student of Western Philosophy must have noticed similarities between Vedanta and the thought of Bishop Berkeley. For Berkeley argued that the world of matter is illusory; that things exist only by virtue of being perceived; and that if we did not perceive them, they would not exist at all were it not for God—or Brahman—who perceives everything all the time.

It is hardly surprising that Crowley was attracted to this mode of thought. It tied in so neatly with Golden Dawn teaching. One could relate Hindu deities, through their characteristics, to those of the West and thus proceed to invoke them. The idea that God manifests through increasingly dense forces and forms, as enunciated in the Qabalah, had its parallel in Vedanta. The Golden Dawn idea that there was an Abyss between the Ideal and the Actual and that there were Three Supernals corresponding to grades of Mastership and, beyond that, Infinity, accorded with the idea that the Universe manifested through Brahma the Creator, Vishnu the Preserver and Shiva the Destroyer, with Brahman, the Ultimate, beyond them. At this point, however, Crowley discovered Buddhism.

It was Allan Bennett who awakened Crowley to the intricacies of Buddhist thought. Crowley proceeded to study classics such as *The Dhammapada* and *The Questions of King Milinda* which he would (again) warmly recommend in later years. Buddhism is the most logically coherent of all the organized religions. It holds that there was a man called Gautama who was born a Hindu Prince. Although his parents did all they could to shield him from the pains of life on earth, he once saw a beggar and this made him so desperately unhappy that he fled his palace in search of truth. Finally, or so it is claimed, he found it.

It is said that after many adventures, Gautama sat beneath the sacred bodhi tree for forty days and forty nights, refusing to move until he had attained to enlightenment. Having achieved

114

this, he was called 'Buddha' by his followers ('Buddha' means 'Enlightened One'). He proclaimed 'Four Noble Truths'; (a) existence is Suffering; (b) the cause of Suffering is Craving; (c) the cessation of Suffering therefore means the cessation of Craving; and (d) the way to achieve that is to follow what Gautama Buddha called 'The Noble Eight-Fold Path'. This consists of eight principles of conduct and mental training.

In addition, Buddha denied a number of beliefs which Hindus hold sacred. He thought that the caste system was utterly ridiculous. Many Westerners would agree; but Gautama went much further. He proceeded to deny both Brahman and atman. In other words, he denied that there was a One behind the Universe and he denied that there is within us a central spirit or soul. Whereas in Hinduism, this spirit or soul goes from body to body through countless incarnations until it finally becomes One with Brahman, in Buddhism there is no soul and there is no One. This is hard to grasp at first—but it is rather like looking at waves on a sea-shore. A wave comes and breaks; it withdraws. Then another wave comes, which may contain much of the same water as before. And then it withdraws and another wave comes. There is no 'central water' in these succeeding waves.

Again, the attentive reader may have noticed a significant parallel in Western Philosophy—Hume. His thought is strikingly similar. In *A Treatise of Human Nature* and *An Enquiry Concerning Human Understanding*, Hume ridiculed the notion of a central 'Self' and regarded beliefs as being simply tendencies of the mind which did not stand up to rational analysis—a position similar to, if not identical with, Buddhist thought. Credit for discerning the similarities between Vedantist thought and Berkeley, and Buddhist thought and Hume, must go to Aleister Crowley, and it is astonishing that this matter is not studied in British Universities.

There are two major forms of Buddhism. The 'Mahayana' or 'Greater Vehicle' is to be found mainly in India, China and Japan, but also Tibet and Nepal. It has blended with the beliefs of the peoples it has influenced. As a result, we find in it the idea that there are many Buddhas or 'Enlightened Ones' and we can pray to them to grant us better lives and better future incarnations—a hypothesis which Gautama, judging from the records, would have found preposterous. In India it is hard to distinguish between Hindu and Mahayana Buddhist beliefs. Nevertheless, the influence of Mahayana has been productive in its fusion with beliefs entertained before its arrival. Results have included a union with Bon so as to produce Tibetan Tantra; and a union with Chinese Taoism so as to produce Cha'an, which became Zen in Japan.

However, this was not the Buddhism which Crowley studied and practised. He went with the 'Hinayana'—also known as 'The Lesser Vehicle' and as 'Theravada'—which is to be found mainly in South-East Asia and most notably Ceylon (now called Sri Lanka). This is the form of Buddhism which is closest to the teaching of Gautama and his immediate disciples. It is also the form Allan Bennett embraced, especially when he entered a Burmese Buddhist monastery as Bhikku Ananda Metteya.

Crowley was so impressed by Buddhist thought of the Hinayana or Theravada school that it temporarily became a dominant part of his intellectual framework—one which we shall be exploring further in Chapter 3. For the time being, it is better to turn our attention from theory to practice.

There are very few books on the practice of Yoga which are worth reading. This is a pity, for Yoga is the Way for Hindus and Buddhists. The goal of the Hindu is to have union with Brahman. The goal of the Buddhist, Mahayana or Hinayana, is Nirvana—cessation of Existence, which is Suffering. Accordingly, the ego must annihilate itself in that union with Nirvana (Nothingness) which is Yoga. Either way, the goal is union with the Infinite.

The essence of the matter is simplicity itself. As Crowley put it: 'Sit still. Stop thinking. Shut up. Get out.' Nothing else is actually needed for the practice of Yoga, but some may require more specific directions. Most texts will confuse more than they clarify. Those written by semi-literate Hindus in the hope of making money and disciples out of gullible Westerners are the worst. The best are those manuals which Crowley studied and recommended: the *Yoga Aphorisms* of Patanjali; *Raja Yoga* by Swami Vivekananda, the great disciple of Ramakrishna; the

Shiva Sanhita; and the *Hathayoga Pradipika.* To these the present writer would add the writings of 'Arthur Avalon' (Sir John Woodruffe); Theos Bernard's *Hatha Yoga*; and a very good little book published by Pelican and called simply *Yoga*, by Ernest Wood. Yet the works of Crowley are ahead of all of these. He became a Master of Yoga.

The teaching received from Allan Bennett resulted in Crowley attaining the trance of Dhyana. Further work over the next five years culminated in the higher trance of Samadhi. This trance was repeated throughout the remainder of Crowley's life.[1]

There are a number ways of doing Yoga. The primary way used by Crowley was 'Raja' or 'Royal' Yoga. This way consists simply of one-pointed concentration upon an object, real or imagined. Crowley's practice resulted in his writing that classic work *Part I* of *Book Four*, which was heavily influenced by Allan Bennett's splendid essay, 'The Training of the Mind'. The essentials of Raja Yoga are stated in Crowley's *Summary:*

Firstly, we still the body by the practice called Asana, and secure its ease and the regularity of its functions by Pranayama (breath-control). Thus no messages from the body will disturb the mind.

Secondly, by Yama and Niyama, we still the emotions and passions, and thus prevent them arising to disturb the mind.

Thirdly, by Pratyahara we analyse the mind yet more deeply, and begin to control and suppress thought in general of whatever nature.

Fourthly, we suppress all other thoughts by a direct concentration upon a single thought. This process, which leads to the highest results, consists of three parts, Dharana, Dhyana, and Samadhi, grouped under a single term Samyama.

The process of Dhyana is described in *Book Four* as follows:

In the course of our concentration *we noticed that the contents of the mind at any moment consisted of two things, and no more:* the Object, variable, and the Subject, invariable, or apparently so. *By success in Dharana the object has been made as invariable as the subject.*

Now the result of this is that the two become one. This phenomenon usually comes as a tremendous shock. It is indescribable even by the masters of language; and it is therefore not surprising that semi-educated stutterers wallow in oceans of gush.

All the poetic faculties and all the emotional faculties are thrown into a sort of ecstasy by an occurrence which overthrows the mind, and makes the rest of life seem absolutely worthless in comparison.

Crowley's mastery of Yoga is demonstrated in his beautifully lucid manuals of practical instruction. *Liber E vel Exercitiorum* teaches Physical Clairvoyance, Asana (Posture), Pranayama (Regularization of the Breathing) and Dharana (Control of Thought)—together with a method of investigating one's physical limitations and a recommended course of reading in a mere seven pages. *Liber RV vel Spiritus* gives detailed teaching in Pranayama in four and a half pages. Nor are Crowley's prescriptions confined solely to the Way of Raja Yoga. *Liber CMXIII,* (also called *Liber Thisharb*) gives instruction in Gnana Yoga, the Yoga of Knowledge, which consists of training the intellect. *Liber Astarte* is probably the finest document extant on Bhakta-Yoga, the Yoga of uniting oneself to a particular Deity by love and devotion. The teaching which Crowley received from a guru in Madras (1905) concerned Tantric and Kundalini Yoga, and we will be returning to this subject in our exploration of Sex-Magick. But one fruitful result was the writing of two manuals for advanced students. *Liber HHH* gives three methods of attainment through complex meditations and its third method, *SSS,* is specifically concerned with the Kundalini—the Serpent Power at the base of the spine—which, when correctly activated, rises to unite with centres of energy within the brain and confer Enlightenment. And *Liber Yod* gives alternative ways of accomplishing the same objective. Throughout his writings on Yoga, Crowley does not waste a word. Methods are set forth with the utmost clarity and simplicity; the rest is left to the student.

Only in *Eight Lectures on Yoga (1939)*, in which Crowley appropriately described himself as Mahatma Guru Sri Paramahansa Shivaji, does he delve into theory and give full expression to his mature understanding.

Yoga is an essential part of Crowley's system and we shall be returning to it in Chapter 10. The experience of Yoga and especially the trance of Dhyana in 1901 were essential factors in Crowley's subsequent thought.

3

Scepticism

The experience of Dhyana made of Crowley a Buddhist and a sceptic. At first sight this statement might appear paradoxical to the average Westerner. Yet there is in fact no contradiction, as Crowley proved in his essay, 'Science and Buddhism', whose object was to demonstrate the essential identity of Buddhist and scientific thought.

Buddhism in its purest form can scarcely be described as a religion at all. It holds that there is no God and there is no soul: Gautama Buddha was simply a man who found a Way to Enlightenment and taught it. As he used to say: 'I have not come to teach whether there is God or whether there is not; whether there is an afterlife or whether there is not. I have come to teach only two things: Suffering and Deliverance from Suffering.' According to the most orthodox Buddhist teachers, there is only Samsara, which is Existence, and Nirvana, which is Non-Existence. Since Existence is Suffering, it follows logically that the cessation of Suffering is Non-Existence (those Western Buddhists who fondly imagine that Nirvana implies some kind of self-conscious bliss are merely demonstrating an illogical and fatuous wish-fulfilment fantasy). Not that there is joy in the inexorable conclusion of the Buddhists. One is reminded again of Crowley's mordant New Year card to his friends and acquaintances during his Buddhist period: 'Wishing you a speedy termination of Existence.'

We are conscious of Existence through the processes of our minds. The object of Yoga—Buddhist meditation is of course

Yoga—is to stop the mind, to stop all consciousness of being an independent 'I'. What is this 'I'? The body? The imagination? The intellect? The emotions? The tendencies of the mind? As Hume pointed out, one cannot even say with Descartes, 'I think, therefore I am.' For what is the 'I' that thinks? All we can say with certainty is: 'There is a thought now.'

Two proverbial and time-honoured ways of putting the above simply are: 'It's all in the mind'; and 'There's nothing good or bad but thinking makes it so.'

Our consciousness consists of a succession of thoughts for which Hume used the terms 'ideas' and 'impressions'. Many of these thoughts, ideas or impressions concern the physical world. It is the task of science to investigate the behaviour of the physical world—though a determined Buddhist sceptic would probably argue that in so doing, we are merely investigating the tendencies of our minds to perceive phenomena in certain ways. Buddhist philosophical psychologists have in fact gone deeply into the classification of states of consciousness—a classification used by Crowley in his pioneering essay, 'The Psychology of Hashish'.

What governs the behaviour of the mind? Crowley's studies and his conversations with the celebrated psychologist, Dr H. Maudesley, led him to argue for a time that all depended on the functioning of the human brain. Also influenced by his early training in the Natural Sciences, for a while he embraced the view that all questions of psychology, Magick and Mysticism could be reduced to problems of Cerebral Neurology. He put this point forcefully in the essay, 'The Initiated Interpretation of Cere-monial Magic'. Here he argued that the spirits and demons evoked by the Magician are simply parts of the brain. Evocation is therefore a matter of stimulating chosen brain cells.

This physiological approach is limited by the substantial difficulties of devising appropriate experiments and was certainly handicapped by the lack of appropriate equipment in the early years of this century. By 1908, when he wrote 'The Psychology of Hashish', Crowley was advocating the method of psychological introspection and he appealed to men of science to become pioneers in the exploration of consciousness, gathering their data from experimentation on themselves with the techniques of

Magick and Yoga and also through the carefully observed use of drugs. This appeal was largely ignored until the 1960s when Doctors Timothy Leary, Richard Alpert, Robert S.De Ropp, John Lilly, Robert Anton Wilson and others proceeded to experiment fearlessly and record their results and hypotheses— to the lasting benefit of all concerned with the expansion of human knowledge.

Even after he accepted *The Book of the Law* in 1909, the scientific method and its accompanying necessary scepticism remained a central part of Crowley's approach. The motto of *The Equinox* was indeed 'The Aim of Religion'; but it was equally 'The Method of Science'. During his life and throughout his writings, Crowley insisted upon a hard-headed attitude to Magick and Yoga. In his last work, *Magick Without Tears*, we find him asserting again and again that words must have precise meaning and exact referents, and he consistently turns to one of his favourite companions, Skeat's *Etymological Dictionary*. One could fill pages with examples of his attitude. Here are just a few:

We can no longer assert any single proposition, unless we guard ourselves by enumerating countless conditions which must be assumed. *(Liber V vel Reguli)*

The experimenter is encouraged to use his own intelligence, and not to rely upon any other person or persons, however distinguished, even among ourselves. *(Liber E vel Exercitiorum)*

1. This book is very easy to misunderstand; readers are asked to use the most minute critical care in the study of it, even as we have done in the preparation. *(Liber O vel Manus et Sagittae)*

43. *Concerning a notable danger of Success*—It may occur that owing to the tremendous power of the Samadhi, overcoming all other memories as it should and does do, that the mind of the devotee may be obsessed, so that he declare his particular deity to be sole God and Lord. This error has been the foundation of all dogmatic religions, and so the cause of

more misery than all other errors combined. *(Liber Astarte)*

Let the Zelator attach no credit to any statements that may have been made throughout the course of this instruction, and reflect that even the counsel which we have given as suitable to the average case may be entirely unsuitable to his own. *(Liber RV vel Spiritus)*

oo. It has not been possible to construct this book on a basis of pure Scepticism. This matters less, as the practice leads to scepticism, and it may be through it. *(Liber Thisharb)*

By such methods, the A∴A∴ intends to make occult science as systematic and scientific as chemistry; to rescue it from the ill repute which, thanks both to the ignorant and dishonest quacks which have prostituted its name, and to the fanatical and narrow minded enthusiasts that have turned it into a fetish, has made it an object of aversion to those very minds whose enthusiasm and integrity make them most in need of its benefits, and most fit to obtain them. *(One Star In Sight)*

As Soror Virakam (Mary d'Este Sturges) wrote in her Note to *Book Four:*

Frater Perdurabo is the most honest of all the great religious teachers. Others have said: 'Believe me!' He says: '*Don't* believe me!' He does not ask for followers; would despise and refuse them. He wants an independent and self-reliant body of students to follow out their own methods of research.

In his essay 'The Soldier and The Hunchback: ? and !', Crowley perceived magical progress as being a series of alternating question marks and exclamation marks. He recommended that the student doubted everything (?) until his scepticism was overwhelmed by the unmistakable rapture of ecstatic experience (!). In due course, it would be time to doubt and question the nature and quality of that experience (?) until a greater ecstasy (!) came like a lightning flash to annihilate that doubt.

In Crowley's case, this lightning flash was *The Book of the Law*.

4

The Book of the Law

In Cairo during the Spring of 1904, a series of strange events happened to a wealthy young man aged 29 who was on an extended honeymoon with his newly-pregnant wife. This young man was experienced in the practice of Magick, though disillusioned by it, and of Yoga, and his attitude could be described as one of scientific Buddhist scepticism. His wife, whom he loved passionately, was a beautiful 'empty-headed woman of society', as he later described her, and she had no interest in Magick, Yoga, Science or Buddhism whatsoever.

On the 14 March the couple moved into a flat in a corner house near the Cairo museum, using the names Prince and Princess Chioa Khan. The wife astonished and disturbed her husband by dazedly repeating the statement: 'They are waiting for you.' On 18 March, she declared that 'He who was waiting was Horus', that her husband had offended Him and that he ought to invoke him and implore his pardon. The man carried out a series of tests based upon traditional Golden Dawn teachings concerning the correspondences of Horus. Although the woman had no knowledge at all of occultism, she guessed correctly every time against total odds of over 21,000,000 to 1. She also took her husband to the Cairo Museum and pointed out the image of Horus in the form of Ra-Hoor-Khuit painted upon a wooden stele of the 26th dynasty. This exhibit bore the number 666, the number of the Beast of *Revelations*. The man was by now sufficiently impressed to obey his wife's instructions and invoke Horus, and he received the message that 'the Equinox of the

Gods' had come. She then told him to enter the magical Temple he had set up at mid-day each day for three days. He did this, and between 12.00 noon and 1.00 pm on 8, 9 and 10 April 1904, *The Book of the Law* was dictated to the man by a being who 'announced himself as Aiwass. According to the scribe, Aiwass seemed to be a tall, dark man in his thirties, well knit, active and strong, with the face of a savage king, and eyes veiled lest their gaze should destroy what they saw. The dress was not Arab; it suggested Assyria or Persia, but very vaguely. I took little note of it, for to me at that time Aiwass was an angel such as I had often seen in visions, a being purely astral.'

The voice of Aiwass possessed 'deep timbre, musical and expressive, its tones solemn, voluptuous, tender, fierce or aught else as suited the mood'.

For five years the man fought against the acceptance of the Book and even lost the manuscript. The contents were repugnant to him. But in 1909, as previously related, Aleister Crowley finally accepted and embraced *The Book of the Law*. It became the guiding principle of his life.

The central doctrines of *The Book of the Law* can be stated simply. First and foremost is the commandment: *Do what thou wilt shall be the whole of the Law*—also reiterated as *thou hast no right but to do thy will*. This does *not* mean 'Do what you want'. It means that within every man and every woman there is a True Will—*The Book of the Law* states that *Every man and every woman is a star*—and that the only serious business of life is to discover our True Will and to do it. As the Ancient Greeks put it: Know Thyself; then Be Thyself. *The word of sin is Restriction* means that everything which inhibits the True Will is evil.

Love is the law, Love under will asserts that the nature of the Law is Love but that this love must be directed by the True Will. As Crowley states in his Old Comment: 'Love under will—no casual pagan love; nor love under fear, as the Christians do. But love magically directed, and used as a spiritual formula'.

The Book of the Law states that a New Aeon has commenced with the utterance of Aiwass. According to Crowley, there have been two previous Aeons for humankind. The Aeon of Isis was characterized by matriarchy and Goddess-worship; the Aeon of

Osiris was characterized by patriarchy and the worship of solar-phallic Gods who died, then rose again—Osiris, Adonis, Attis, Dionysus and Jesus Christ; and we are now in the Aeon of Horus, the Crowned and Conquering Child. *The Book of the Law* prophesies that the old Aeon of Osiris will be destroyed and that the planet will be bathed in blood. Barbarism is predicted and the destruction of all Christian sentiments. The Aeon of Horus with its Law of Thelema— the Greek word for Will—will last for roughly two thousand years, and then:

> Hrumachis shall arise and the double-wanded one assume my throne and place. Another prophet shall arise, and bring fresh fever from the skies; another woman shall awake the lust & worship of the Snake; another soul of God and beast shall mingle in the globed priest; another sacrifice shall stain the tomb; another king shall reign; and blessing no longer be poured To the Hawk-headed mystical Lord!'

The cosmology of *The Book of the Law* is of interest to anyone fascinated by Einstein's Theory of Relativity. Infinite Space is called the Goddess NUIT. The force within the atom, that Point which is infinitely small yet omnipresent, is called the God HADIT. This is the God within us. As HADIT declares through Aiwass in the second chapter: 'In the sphere I am everywhere the centre, as she, the circumference, is nowhere found.' The manifested Universe is conceived as being the result of the constant interplay of Nuit and Hadit, or Matter and Energy— though matter is, of course, simply another form of Energy. This interplay is sexual in nature, hence 'Love is the Law, love under will.' One thinks of the Tantrics and their conception of the Universe as resulting from the continuous copulation of Shiva and Shakti, or whichever names are used. From the point of view of planet Earth, the most important conjunction between Nuit and Hadit—the female and the male, the infinitely great and the infinitely small—results in Ra-Hoor-Khuit, the most active form of Horus, God of War, Lord of the present Aeon, the Crowned and Conquering Child, who manifests in two ways, active and passive. As has been stated, Ra-Hoor-Khuit is the most extreme, active form; one could describe it as being the ultimate in projected male energy. In its passive mode, this energy is described as Hoor-Paar-Kraat, whom the ancient Greeks called Harpocrates and who is usually pictured as a Babe in an Egg of Light with his thumb in his mouth, to symbolize Wisdom in Silence.

Aiwass describes himself as 'the Minister of Hoor-Paar-Kraat' and as such—so Thelemites believe—voices the divine message. There is nothing unusual about this, if one examines the history of sacred books which are believed to have been dictated by praeter-human intelligences. The classic example is *The Qu'ran*— also called *The Koran*—and Muslims accept the account of its origins given by its scribe, the former camel-driver who became the Prophet Mohammed. Mohammed stated that he was visited by the Angel Gabriel, Minister of Allah (the Arabic word for 'God') and that during the various visitations, Gabriel dictated the Word of Allah to Mohammed, who wrote down all he heard. Although the putative Word of God is currently being blasphemed by, for instance, the repulsive Ayatollah Khomenei (whose embrace of barbarous ignorance has rendered him incapable of remembering that torture is expressly forbidden in *The Qu'ran*), it cannot be denied that this holy book resulted in a magnificent revival of learning, art, science and civilization along with new discoveries which were a vital contribution to human knowledge. Moreover, the language and poetry of *The Qu'ran* in the original Arabic are so sublime that this book became the foundation stone for the rules of Arabic poetry, to the delight of all lovers of true art. The claims made by the many millions of Muslims regarding *The Qu'ran* are similar to those made by Thelemites—'who calls us Thelemites will do no wrong'—with regard to *The Book of the Law*.

In the first chapter, Aiwass reveals the utterance of Nuit. In the second, we hear the statements of Hadit. In the third, we have the words of Ra-Hoor-Khuit.

Aleister Crowley is hailed as the Prophet, The Beast 666 come to destroy the Old Aeon. He is enjoined to appoint a 'Scarlet Woman' for 'Now ye shall know that the chosen priest and apostle of infinite space is the prince-priest, the Beast; and in his

Aleister Crowley encased in 'the bomb-proof armour of the English aristocracy', a line he used in his novel *Moonchild*.

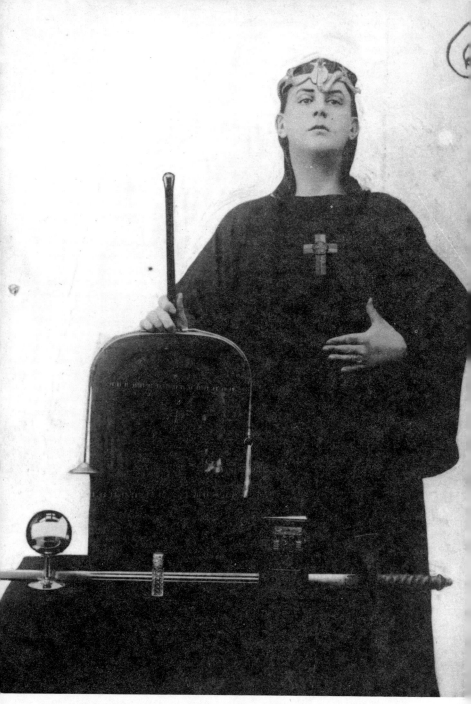

Photograph first published in *Book Four*, 1913. The magician stands with all weapons to hand and works 'with eternity at my command and omnipotence at my disposal'.

A stage magician – the Great Mysterioso. Also Prince Chioa Khan at the time of receiving *The Book of the Law*.

Jan: 10th 1910

A very nice Edwardian family snapshot. The man is the Beast 666, Rose served as his Scarlet Woman, the little girl is their daughter Lola Zaza, and the photograph was taken on the day of their divorce in 1910.

Leah Hirsig — Alostrael — the Scarlet Woman. (Rose and Leah were the Beast's greatest loves.) 'Paint me as a dead soul,' Leah said.

A lawyer, the Beast and a Scarlet Woman go to court for Crowley versus Constable and Co, 1934. Crowley is clearly determined not to let the side down.

Muslims have their prophet in Mohammed. Thelemites have theirs in the Master Therion.

The Winston Churchill of Magick.

woman called the Scarlet Woman is all power given. They shall gather my children into their fold: they shall bring the glory of the stars into the hearts of men.' This unexpected appointment was one major reason why Crowley rejected *The Book of the Law* for five years. He did not wish to be thrust into the role of Great Prophet and perceived that belief as being evidence of gross delusion.

There are other reasons why he fought against *The Book of the Law*. As a Shelleyan humanist, he was repelled by its exaltation of elitism and violence. As a Buddhist, he could not accept that 'existence is pure joy'. As a late Victorian gentleman, he did not welcome the imminent collapse of civilization. As an intelligent scholar, he disliked the idea of revelations from mysterious, supernatural sources. Finally, as we have seen, he was moved to take it seriously and it became the most important thing in his life. But how seriously should *we* take *The Book of the Law*? Those who are tempted to laugh come upon the following lines:

Begone! ye mockers; even though ye laugh in my humour ye shall laugh not long: then when ye are sad know that I have forsaken you.
He that is righteous shall be righteous still; he that is filthy shall be filthy still.

One thing can be said with absolute certainty: 'Yet to all it shall seem beautiful. Its enemies who say not so, are mere liars.'

One finds many gems in this extraordinary work. For example, in contemplating the notion that the God—or personified force—which rules the present Aeon is the hawk-headed Horus, one is reminded of Zoroaster's statement in *The Chaldean Oracles*—'God is He with the head of a Hawk, having a spiral force'—and thus led on to the idea advanced by bio-chemists, that the original force of evolution is DNA, which is spiral.

Many of the verses in *The Book of the Law* are plain as paint; others are very difficult to understand. Although Crowley himself studied the Book devoutly from 1909 until his life ended in 1947, he died accepting the sentence: 'Ye, even ye, know not this meaning all.'

Certain prophecies came true—e.g., 'There cometh a rich man from the West who shall pour his gold upon thee.' This was Karl J. Germer, who supported Crowley financially and succeeded him as 'Outer Head' of the Ordo Templi Orientis. Moreover,

> This book shall be translated into all tongues: but always with the original in the writing of the Beast; for in the chance shape of the letters and their position to one another: in these are mysteries that no Beast shall divine. Let him not seek to try: but one cometh after him, whence I say not, who shall discover the Key of it all. Then this line drawn is a key: then this circle squared in its failure is a key also. And Abrahadabra. It shall be his child & that strangely. Let him not seek after this; for thereby alone can he fall from it.

According to Crowley, this refers to his 'magical son', Charles Stansfield Jones, Frater Achad, whose Qabalistic workings demonstrated the key numbers on which the work is based. For there are many technical mysteries in *The Book of the Law*, which lie beyond the scope of this elementary work. It suffices to say that practising Magicians and Qabalists who check the use of numbers and letters pronounce themselves to be satisfied with the ideas advanced.

One prophecy which has yet to be fulfilled is that which reads:

> Change not as much as the style of a letter; for behold! thou, o prophet, shalt not behold all these mysteries hidden therein.
> The child of thy bowels, *he* shall behold them.
> Expect him not from the East, nor from the West; for from no expected house cometh that child. Aum!

The present writer brought *The Book of the Law* into an historical work, published in the UK in 1980 as *Hitler and the Age of Horus*, in the USA as *Hitler: The Occult Messiah* (1981) and subsequently in Japanese translation (1985). Among many other points—for instance, the contention that Hitler and some of his associates were involved in a blasphemous parody of the

132

true principles of Magick, from which they derived both their success and their failure—it was argued that *The Book of the Law* offers the most accurate predictive insight into the breakdown of nineteenth-century rational-humanist civilization. It remains to be seen how many more statements contained in the Book turn out to be true, especially:

> I am the warrior Lord of the Forties: the Eighties cower before me, & are abased.

And:

> Hail! ye twin warriors about the pillars of the world! for your time is nigh at hand.

Certainly Crowley came to hold that the old civilization was breaking down in repeated cataclysms of violence, war and bloodshed. Neither the First nor the Second World Wars surprised him. And if human stupidity surmounts human intelligence, as it currently shows every sign of doing, then one can sadly and despairingly predict a Third.

We shall be returning to these considerations in Part Three. For the present it is best to give the reader a taste of *The Book of the Law* with short extracts from its three chapters:

I, 61–65 (Nuit):

> But to love me is better than all things: if under the night-stars in the desert thou presently burnest mine incense before me, invoking me with a pure heart, and the Serpent flame therein, thou shalt come a little to lie in my bosom. For one kiss wilt thou then be willing to give all; but whoso gives one particle of dust shall lose all in that hour. Ye shall gather goods and store of women and spices; ye shall wear rich jewels; ye shall exceed the nations of the earth in splendour & pride; but always in the love of me, and so shall ye come to my joy. I charge you earnestly to come before me in a single robe, and covered with a rich head-dress. I love you! I yearn to you! Pale or purple, veiled or voluptuous, I who am all pleasure and purple, and drunkenness of the innermost sense, desire you. Put on the

wings, and arouse the coiled splendour within you: come unto me!

At all my meetings with you shall the priestess say—and her eyes shall burn with desire as she stands bare and rejoicing in my secret temple—To me! To me! calling forth the flame of the hearts of all in her love-chant.

Sing the rapturous love-song unto me! Burn to me perfumes! Wear to me jewels! Drink to me, for I love you! I love you!

I am the blue-lidded daughter of Sunset; I am the naked brilliance of the voluptuous night-sky.

To me! To me!

The Manifestation of Nuit is at an end.

II, 22–24 (Hadit):

I am the Snake that giveth Knowledge & Delight and bright glory, and stir the hearts of men with drunkenness. To worship me take wine and strange drugs whereof I will tell my prophet, & be drunk thereof! They shall not harm ye at all. It is a lie, this folly against self. The exposure of innocence is a lie. Be strong, o man! lust, enjoy all things of sense and rapture: fear not that any God shall deny thee for this.

I am alone: there is no God where I am.

Behold! these be grave mysteries; for there are also of my friends who be hermits. Now think not to find them in the forest or on the mountain; but in beds of purple, caressed by magnificent beasts of women with large limbs, and fire and light in their eyes, and masses of flaming hair about them; there shall ye find them. Ye shall see them at rule, at victorious armies, at all the joy; and there shall be in them a joy a million times greater than this. Beware lest any force another, King against King! Love one another with burning hearts; on the low men trample in the fierce lust of your pride, in the day of your wrath.

III, 48–61 (Ra-Hoor-Khuit):

I am in a secret fourfold word, the blasphemy against all gods of men.

Curse them! Curse them! Curse them!

With my Hawk's head I peck at the eyes of Jesus as he hangs upon the cross.

I flap my wings in the face of Mohammed & blind him.

With my claws I tear out the flesh of the Indian and Buddhist, Mongol and Din.

Bahlasti! Ompehda! I spit on your crapulous creeds.

Let Mary inviolate be torn upon wheels; for her sake let all chaste women be utterly despised among you!

Also for beauty's sake and love's!

Despise also all cowards; professional soldiers who dare not fight, but play: all fools despise!

But the keen and the proud, the royal and the lofty; ye are brothers!

As brothers fight ye!

There is no law beyond Do what thou wilt.

There is an end of the word of the God enthroned in Ra's seat, lightening the girders of the soul.

Small wonder that Crowley, hailed in *The Book of the Law* as Ankh-f-n-khonsu, priest of the Princes, finally wrote 'The Comment' which is both a challenge to those who have sufficient courage, and a prohibition upon long, boring commentaries on commentaries (the fate of most sacred texts)—and on squabbles, quibbles and persecution among those called Thelemites, whose desire is to do their Wills in the Aeon into which this planet has entered during its spin through the agony of evolving consciousness.

THE COMMENT

Do what thou wilt shall be the whole of the Law.

The study of this Book is forbidden. It is wise to destroy this copy after the first reading.

Whosoever disregards this does so at his own risk and peril. These are most dire.

Those who discuss the contents of this Book are to be shunned by all, as centres of pestilence.

All questions of the Law are to be decided only by appeal to my writings, each for himself.

There is no law beyond Do what thou wilt.

Love is the law, love under will.

The priest of the princes.

Ankh-f-n-khonsu.

5

Poetry and Mysticism

It is greatly to be regretted that very few people care for poetry in England today, even though this country has in the past produced so many of the world's greatest poets. Consequently, my remarks on Crowley's poetry will be brief.

Until 1914 Crowley was taken seriously as a poet and his work was reviewed, as will be recalled, in the leading journals of the day. Austin Harrison, editor of *The English Review*, called him 'England's greatest living poet'. Two factors conspired to prevent Crowley from receiving his just share of recognition. Firstly, there were the changes in poetic expression and fashion which occurred after the First World War, and which resulted in his work being disparaged as old-fashioned and outmoded. Secondly, there was the campaign of personal vilification, which led to stupidity and prejudice even on the part of quite sensible critics. J. F. C. Fuller and, much later, Charles Richard Cammell—himself a poet of notable technical facility— might insist on the many virtues of Crowley's verse; but few bothered to listen. Fortunately, there are currently signs of a change in attitude. Martin Booth, a recognized poet and scholar, has recently edited and introduced a volume entitled *Selected Poems* (Crucible 1986) and although the principles of Mr Booth's selection are occasionally puzzling, he is to be congratulated for what may turn out to be a courageous first step towards a sound revaluation. This is sorely required, for all lovers of good poetry who investigate the matter without prejudice are bound to discover truth, beauty, versatility and admirable technical virtuosity in Crowley's poetical works.

Certainly there are faults and these are particularly evident in the earlier writings. Like all dedicated artists he set out to learn from the masters of the past and one finds many echoes of Shelley, Browning and Swinburne, which leave the young Crowley open to the charge of plagiarism. As Somerset Maugham pointed out in his Introduction to the second edition of his early novel *The Magician*, one might think that the line: 'It's rather hard, isn't it, sir, to make sense of it?', was written by Browning, when in fact it was Aleister Crowley. However, the result of Crowley's alleged plagiarism in stylistic terms was that he became adept in a wide variety of techniques of versification and developed into a master of the poet's craft. Of course, craftsmanship alone, essential and necessary condition though it is, does not make for great poetry. Too many of the poems published in *The Collected Works* (1905–7) display faultless technical skill yet make for wearisome reading. One wishes that Crowley had either written less or printed less. Even so, just as we judge Coleridge by *Kubla Khan* rather than *Ode To An Ass*, so it should be with Crowley.

Our difficulties are increased by the fact that frequently Crowley is not an easy poet to read, for he wrote in the full expectation that his readers were highly educated and literate, fully aware of the poets before him and intimately acquainted with the Greek and Latin classics and mythology as well as the Bible. Fortunately, not all of his poetry is quite so intellectually demanding.

> The world for a whore!
> The sky for a harlot!
> All life-at your door
> For a woman of scarlet!
>
> I'll give that and more
> In this planet of boredom
> For a girl that's a whore
> And is proud of her whoredom!

'Lines which Sedley or Suckling might have written,' as Cammell rightly comments. Louis Wilkinson was particularly fond of the line: 'O English girl! Half baby and half bitch.'

Here it is only possible to state my opinion that Crowley is one of the greatest poets in the English language and to support this opinion by recommending examples to the interested reader. Those who like witty, elegant satire in rhyming couplets should try *The Fun of the Fair*. Those who prefer the rhyming couplet to be employed for serious intellectual purposes should take up *The Sword of Song* in *The Collected Works Volume II*, in which Christianity is savaged and Buddhism expounded and analysed. Those who enjoy rhapsody will find it in *The City of God*. The lyrics in *Alice: An Adultery* have enchanted some. In *AHA* one finds Magick, Yoga and *The Book of the Law* advocated and explained brilliantly and beautifully. There are few, if any, cries of magical ecstasy as powerful as the *Hymn to Pan*. For exquisite love poetry, one should turn to the four *Odes To The Rose: Rosa Mundi, Rosa Coeli, Rosa Inferni* and the agony of *Rosa Decidua*. Other poems have been noted and praised earlier in this work but *Leah Sublime* deserves to be singled out. This extraordinary poem has been condemned as merely an exercise in obscenity by the dull and dirty-minded, but is in fact a Tantra and a holy work. Here, like Rabelais, in a glorious act of poetic alchemy Crowley suggests the highest conceptions by using the gross as his vehicle.

His poetic gifts remain relevant when we turn our attention to the second subject of this chapter: Mysticism. Mysticism is the transcending of intellectual boundaries in a union with the Infinite. It is argued by mystics and was argued by Crowley that if rational thought is pursued far enough, it ends in self-contradiction. A similar conclusion can be reached by the study of Berkeley, Hume and Kant in the Western philosophical tradition. In other words, we cannot apprehend ultimate truth about the Infinite by the use of the finite intellect. We will have to use methods which unleash other faculties of the brain.

All statements concerning Mysticism—other than denials of its validity—fall into two categories: the prescriptive and the descriptive. Prescriptive statements recommend or exhort courses of action; they say: 'Do x', and we have already looked at the excellence of Crowley's writings here. Descriptive statements expound the experience of the subject. They might be highly specific—e.g., 'I saw a red rose, heard a bell chime once, smelled burning wood and felt a piercing pain in my heart.' Or they might be vague and woolly—e.g., 'I was bathed in a vibrating ocean of God's love.' Unfortunately, the statements of too many mystics are of the latter variety. It is very hard to express the inexpressible, to translate what is beyond reason into the words of reason. It is like describing sight to one born blind or orgasm to a six year old. Many mystics lack literary ability—there is no reason why they should have it—and this makes the task even more difficult than it already is. Crowley's advantage was that as a great poet, he was a master of language.

> Had I a million songs,
> And every song a million words,
> And every word a million meanings,
> I could not count the choral throngs
> Of Beauty's beatific birds,
> Or gather up the paltry gleanings
> Of this great harvest of delight!
> Hast thou not heard the words aright?
> That world is truly infinite. . . .

He used his literary gifts, among other things, to express his many and varied states of mystical consciousness. We can read his descriptions in *AHA*, from which the above quotation is taken, and beyond all else, *The Holy Books*. In *The Book of the Heart Girt with a Serpent*, one will come upon passages such as the following:

Weary, weary! saith the scribe. Who shall lead me to the sight of the Rapture of my master?
The body is weary and the soul is sore weary and sleep weighs down their eyelids; yet ever abides the sure consciousness of ecstasy, unknown, yet known in that its being is certain. O Lord, be my helper, and bring me to the bliss of the Beloved.

All day I sing of Thy delight. All night I delight in Thy song. There is no other day or night than this.

The rest is silence.

6

Sex-Magick

Sex Magicians are those who believe that sexual union between Man and Woman is the holiest act on Earth of which human beings are capable (it may even be the holiest act in the Universe)—and that this act can be used for magical purposes as defined earlier. (There are also those who make similar claims for homosexuality.) How did this belief come about?

It is a very old belief which we find in a wide variety of African, Middle Eastern and Asian cultures. Well over two thousand years ago, certain Hindu sects proceeded to make a precise science and a delicate art out of the intentional use of sexual energy and it is this which we know by the term Tantric Yoga. Subsequently, certain Buddhist sects adopted these techniques, mated them with Tibetan Bon practices and introduced their own technical variations. This matter, and the differences between the Hindu and the Buddhist approaches can be studied with profit in an excellent work called *Tantra For Westerners: A Practical Guide* by Francis King.

The use of sexual energies for the enhancement and evolution of consciousness appears to be as old as civilized humanity itself. Nor is this surprising when one considers the interesting fact that on Earth, the creatures with the highest intelligence mate most often. Only the intellectual fatuity and moral dishonour of Christianity, with its contemptible notions of sin and guilt vis-à-vis the exercise of natural functions, has caused people to become morbidly hysterical over what may turn out, on reasoned analysis, to be sheer common sense.

It has been argued by some occultists that there has always been a Western tradition of wisdom concerning the use of sex in bringing the human spirit to consciousness of its innate divinity. Their writings cite quite a number of groups and movements: various pagan cults; the witches; the alchemists; the Knights Templar; the Rosicrucians; the Illuminati; the Freemasons; and so on. Orthodox historians with impeccable scholarly credentials have disputed these contentions. This is neither the time nor the place to enter into this particular debate, though it seems reasonable to remark that given the interchange of information between East and West over the past two thousand years via the Mediterranean and other trade routes, and given the ancient nature of the belief in sexual magic and the existence of Tantric sects in the Indian sub-continent, it is not impossible that certain couples or groups practised certain sexual techniques which they passed on to their successors.

At some point towards the end of the nineteenth century, Karl Kellner, a wealthy German iron-master, claimed to have received teaching in techniques of sexual magick from two Indians and one Arab. Even as simple a matter as this has been, and still is, disputed; Kellner's source may have been Western, so some historians have argued. What is not in dispute, however, is the fact that Kellner set up an Order called the Ordo Templi Orientis (OTO) or Order of the Templars of the East, on the basis of a suspect charter from the world of fringe Masonry; and that in its higher degrees, the OTO taught Sex-Magick to its initiates.

One sometimes wonders why historical truth regarding magical orders is so difficult, if not impossible, to ascertain. A far more ancient lineage has been claimed for the OTO in some quarters, including a line from the Sufis via the Knights Templar, then through Freemasonry and the Illuminati of Adam Weishaupt, and various other organizations which are usually cited in any attempt to prove an ancient pedigree for a modern Order. Perhaps the origins of the OTO do go back to eighteenth-century Germany or even to the medieval Knights Templar; but I am not aware of any documentary evidence which could establish the truth of these assertions. Moreover, even the late nineteenth-century Masonic status claimed for and by the OTO is questionable. If I understand the position correctly, United Grand Lodge—the foremost body of English-speaking Freemasonry, honoured by Freemasons throughout the world—regards the Masonic claims of the OTO as being dubious if not downright spurious. However, it is hardly my intention here to examine a matter best left to Masons.

Karl Kellner died in 1904 or 1905 (once again, accounts vary) and Mr Kenneth Grant has even stated baldly, without any supporting evidence, that Kellner died 'in mysterious circumstances'. Thankfully, we are at last in the realm of hard facts in stating that his successor as 'Outer Head of the Order' was another German, Theodor Reuss. Reuss was involved in the curious world of fringe Masonry and was also an agent of the German Secret Service. But the OTO seems to have grown steadily under his leadership and published a journal called *The Oriflamme*. For a time, the founder of the Anthroposophical Society, Rudolf Steiner, was a member of the OTO.

Aleister Crowley came into contact with Reuss and the OTO in 1910 in the following way. When he started publishing Golden Dawn rituals in his periodical *The Equinox*, 'MacGregor' Mathers served him with an injunction restraining publication. Mr Justice Bucknill confirmed the injunction. Crowley appealed, won, and enjoyed the resulting publicity.

> As a side issue, Mathers having claimed in court to be the Chief of the Rosicrucian Order, I was invaded by an innumerable concourse of the queerest imaginable people, each of whom independently asserted that he himself, and he alone, was that Chief. Having my own information on the subject, though communicating it to nobody else, I got rid of these pests as quickly as possible. One of my callers, however, did show some method in his madness; a man named Theodor Reuss....
> *(The Confessions)*

Crowley joined the OTO knowing nothing of the teachings to the highest initiates and thought no more of the matter, regarding the Order merely as 'a convenient compendium of the more important truths of freemasonry'. But in 1912 he received another surprise visit from Reuss, who accused him of publishing the supreme magical secret of the Order.

> I protested that I knew no such secret. He said 'But you have printed it in the plainest language'. I said that I could not have done so because I did not know it. He went to the bookshelves; taking out a copy of *The Book of Lies*, he pointed to a passage in the... chapter. It instantly flashed upon me. The entire symbolism not only of Free Masonry but of many other traditions blazed upon my spiritual vision. From that moment the OTO assumed its proper importance in my mind. I understood that I held in my hands the key to the future progress of humanity. (*The Confessions*)

Crowley's views on the connection between Magick/Yoga and sexuality prior to the visit of Reuss are most succinctly stated in Part 1 of *Book Four*:

> The only difficult question is that of continence, which is complicated by many considerations, such as that of energy; but everybody's mind is hopelessly muddled on this subject, which some people confuse with erotology, and others with sociology. There will be no clear thinking on this matter until it is understood as being solely a branch of athletics.

Yet there is evidence in earlier writings that on many occasions he intuitively suspected that there is a vital connection between sexual energies and magical working. After all, *The Book of the Law* is, among other things, a Tantric text: the Universe manifests through the perpetual love-making of Nuit and Hadit. Through the agency of Theodor Reuss' reference to a chapter in *The Book of Lies*—a chapter which Crowley had scribbled hastily in a mood of disgust—the Beast finally perceived the vital importance of Sex Magick and realized that the OTO was in possession of practical techniques. Reuss initiated him into the highest degrees of the Order, gave him such wisdom as he had and made him 'Supreme and Holy King' of the English-speaking section he was requested to found.

146

For this task, Crowley took the name Baphomet—the idol worshipped by the original Knights Templar, according to their enemies in the Church. He devoted himself to establishing the Order in England, rewrote the rituals so as to introduce magical initiation into what had originally been purely masonic ceremonies, rewrote the sexual instructions for the higher degrees and recruited members. *The Equinox* became the official organ of the OTO as well as the A∴A∴. Baphomet chartered an American branch of the Order under Charles Stansfield Jones. There is every reason to believe that the English-speaking section would have grown, prospered and flourished if the Treasurer had not become insane, robbed the Order of its funds and alienated Boleskine, the valuable property donated by Crowley.

In 1922 Reuss resigned and nominated Crowley as his successor. The majority of German Lodges confirmed Baphomet as Outer Head of the Order a few years later. Crowley continued to do OTO work until his death, by which time the major centre of its activity was California. The subsequent history of the Order will be related in Part Five.

Naturally Crowley investigated techniques of Sex Magick with his customary thoroughness and enthusiasm. Consequently, there are a variety of his writings which set forth his experiments, conclusions and instructions. His *Diaries* give us the raw material of his experience. 'Energised Enthusiasm', a splendid essay published in *The Equinox* and subsequently in *Gems From The Equinox*, is the best introduction to the subject: one recalls his point that the sailor's cry for Wine, Woman and Song is simply a crude way of invoking Dionysus, Aphrodite and Apollo. *De Arte Magica* and *Liber Agape*, documents originally entrusted only to the highest OTO initiates, impart the OTO techniques and these are illuminated by his comments. Other subtle methods for the advanced students—for they are couched in veiled language—are to be found in two *Holy Books*, printed in *Magick: In Theory and Practice* and *Gems From The Equinox: Liber Cheth vel Vallum Abiegni* expounds the secret of the Holy Graal; and *Liber A'ash vel Capricorni Pneumatici* that of the Sacred Lance. The reader may possibly object to the use of these technical terms and the objection is valid. The trouble is the difficulty of putting

147

abstruse matters in plain language, a hardship of which scientists never tire of complaining. It is rather like trying to explain nuclear physics to the layman whose acquaintance with mathematics ended with the passing of a school examination. However, it can be said that the interested reader will go far towards comprehension of the essential points if it is borne in mind that the Holy Graal on Earth is the vagina and the Sacred Lance is the penis.

The method Crowley gives in *Liber Stellae Rubeae* is perhaps the most succinct and technically sound expression of the essence of the matter, although it is difficult to perform it well. *The Paris Working*, which one would like to see published in an easily available edition but extracts from which have been printed in Crowley's *The Book of Thoth*, gives a record of homosexual experimentation which is of surpassing interest to those who are inclined to this mode.

Those who require perspectives other than those of Crowley are recommended to turn to four works. The last chapter in Israel Regardie's admirable *The Tree of Life* refers to something called 'The Mass of the Holy Ghost' and gives sterling technique couched in alchemical language; no genuine student of alchemy should experience much difficulty of interpretation. In *The Magical World of Aleister Crowley*, Francis King informs the beginner how he or she may start on Sex Magick with the commendable clarity which distinguishes his work; and the same author gives more advanced but absolutely safe methods in his *Tantra For Westerners: A Practical Guide*, which was recommended earlier for its learned exposition of Eastern philosophy and practice. In *A Manual of Sex Magick*, a curious and at times unintentionally hilarious work, Louis T. Culling advocated methods which derive from the OTO and Crowley as formulated by an American ex-disciple of the latter, C. F. Russell: there are differences of technique here, but the practices are fundamentally sound. Finally, there is *Liber XXXVI: The Star Sapphire*, a short ritual which is to be found in *MAGICK: In Theory And Practice* and which was originally published in *The Book of Lies*. This is still a matter for debate among Sex Magicians.

In *The Confessions*, Crowley states that when Reuss accused

148

him of publishing the secret of the OTO, the latter proved his case by opening *The Book of Lies* at Chapter 36, 'The Star Sapphire', which begins: 'Let the Adept be armed with his Magick Rood (and provided with his Mystic Rose).' As is pointed out in Crowley's *Magick Without Tears*, this issues in a puzzle: the incident described unquestionably took place in 1912; yet *The Book of Lies* was only published in 1913.

In endeavouring to make sense of this bizarre event, one is confronted by the following possibilities:

1. Theodor Reuss and Aleister Crowley were in some extraordinary time-warp. This seems unlikely.
2. *The Book of Lies* was in fact published in 1912, not 1913, and the date on the title page of the first edition is wrong. Again, this seems unlikely. One would expect the author, publisher and printer to get the year right.
3. Crowley's memory, though usually excellent, was faulty here and Reuss was referring not to *The Book of Lies* but to some other work.
4. Since Crowley swore to Reuss that he would never publicly betray the secret of the OTO and kept that oath, his statements about *The Star Sapphire* in *The Confessions* and *Magick Without Tears* are a blind.

The third and fourth points of view were argued by the late Israel Regardie in disputation with the present writer. He insisted that *Liber Stellae Rubae* was the work referred to by Reuss; and that *The Star Sapphire* was what Crowley's Commentary in the second and subsequent editions of *The Book of Lies* stated it to be—a revised version of a simple, basic and essential ceremony taught in the Golden Dawn and known as The Lesser Banishing Ritual of the Hexagram. One can only respect the magical experience and opinions of Dr Regardie. But others, including the present writer, have found *The Star Sapphire* to be highly effective when performed as a holy rite of Sexual Magick.

Some readers may be in danger of losing patience at this point on account of the technicalities involved. We must therefore return to basics. Why do Sex Magick? How does one go about it? And what are the likely results?

One does Sex Magick in order to evolve, since, as stated

earlier, 'Magick is the Science and Art of realising the divine self by changing the human self.'

As to procedure, one can make a decent start, if one is a man, by concentrating on the divine essence rather than the personality of the woman to whom one is making love, and vice-versa. It is important to keep this concentration one-pointed, as in Yoga. The man should surrender his ego to the Goddess within the woman and the woman should surrender hers to the God within the man. It is technically advantageous for the man and woman to identify with a God and a Goddess to whom they are attracted, and it does not matter from which belief-system the God and the Goddess are taken—though it helps if the man and the woman draw on similar mythologies. This simple and enjoyable practice should enhance sex, even if it achieves nothing else, and will enable novices, if they are interested, to approach more advanced methods, as indicated in the writings recommended, with a comprehension possible only to those with practical experience of the subject.

The likely results are, to begin with, a greater joy in sexuality; an improved understanding of the word 'love'; possibly thoughts on the nature of the interaction between Matter and Energy in the Universe for those intellectually inclined; and a greater awareness of the miracle of Life.

More advanced practices, undertaken sincerely and diligently, will in all probability lead to extraordinary and perhaps, on occasion, disturbing, but nevertheless ecstatic states of consciousness.

Crowley's contribution to the science and art of Sex Magick consisted in dedicated and persistent experimentation which enabled him to write fine manuals of technique and exalted works enabling others to expand and develop their own consciousness. In his time and on account of the oath he swore to Reuss, these techniques were available only to high grade OTC initiates. But the works which contain them can now be obtained by anyone with sufficient desire to hunt them down.[1] Detailed criticism of these methods by Hindu or Buddhist Tantric Adepts would of course be valuable; yet perhaps their methods are more suited to the East, and Crowley deserves credit for bringing these

150

to the West in a form better suited to our time and place.

He did not claim to be anything more than a pioneer and many failures are recorded in his Diaries (that is to say that the operation did not achieve what he intended it to accomplish). But his work here is a vital part of his legacy. It is likely that in the future others will build upon it and extend his methods to fields unsuspected even by him, thus enabling a further expansion of human intelligence, awareness and consciousness of the Universe and our place in it. This is a development which he would have warmly welcomed. For, as his fascinating contemporary, the artist and magician Austin Osman Spare aptly remarked about the nature of Life: 'All things fornicate all the time.'

Note

1. In the principal appendix to *Crowley on Christ*, edited by Francis King, the interested reader can find Crowley's '*De Arte Magica*', a commentary on his *Liber Agape*, a principal appendix to *Secret Rituals of the OTO*, again edited by Francis King. The subect of these is, of course, technical Sex Magick, and to this end, in *De Arte Magica*, Crowley quotes the ritual of the Star Sapphire in full.

   With all respect to the memory of my great, late friend, Dr Israel Regardie, I think that on this one issue, his customary wisdom and acute powers of perception were distinguished by their absence – unless he was adhering to some oath sworn once upon a time to preserve certain secrets and mislead enquirers.

   Today, there is no point at all in secrecy over these issues. The fact is that Crowley pointed out the Star Sapphire to OTO initiates because it contains the essence of the matter, as every man and woman who have performed it would agree.

7

Drugs

Mankind appears always to have used drugs to alter consciousness. Superficial observers have discerned here nothing more
than a desire to escape from reality, yet they utterly fail to define
the term 'reality'. They also fail to consider the fact that in
primitive tribes, the shaman or medicine man who is responsible
for the relations of the tribe with God or the Gods frequently uses
drugs in order to attain divine communion. In primitive cultures,
drugs are regarded as sacred substances.

Drugs can be used or abused. There seems to be little point, for
instance, in becoming 'blind drunk' on alcohol other than to
anaesthetize oneself from emotional pain; yet too many do this
too often. Others, however, employ alcohol to enhance
enjoyment, consciousness and social interaction (hence the
statement of Rabelais: 'By wine is Man made divine.').
Marijuana is taken by some to bring about euphoria and
heightened awareness; and by others in order to drift into a state
of tedious vacuity. Some imbibe LSD for no reason other than to
plunge into an unprofitable chaos of undifferentiated sensation;
others, such as Dr John Lilly, take it to engage in complex
explorations of consciousness. Both Lilly and Dr Timothy Leary
argue that human beings can be regarded as biological computers
and that LSD can be used to induce states in which we become
aware of our programming and can then re-programme
ourselves in order to function more effectively.

In fact, there are essentially three purposes for which drugs are
taken: (a) to kill pain; (b) to increase sensory enjoyment; (c) to

explore consciousness and augment one's awareness of the Universe. Crowley was familiar with all of these motivations.

It will be recalled that he was introduced to mind-expanding drugs by Allan Bennett in London 1899. The latter took a variety of substances—particularly opium, morphine, cocaine and chloroform—partly to relieve his asthma and partly to 'open the veils of matter'. He also insisted on scrupulous scientific observation: the dose and the results had to be meticulously noted. Six years later, Crowley returned to serious experimentation with hashish and his early experiences with Bennett proved invaluable.

At that time, mind-expanding drugs were legal. Crowley used to go to E. P. Whineray, a chemist in Stafford Street, off Old Bond Street, and purchase whatever he wanted over the counter—a procedure which is somewhat more civilized than the illegal, sleazy dealings of our own days. One major consequence of Crowley's drug-taking was his essay, 'The Psychology of Hashish'.

Here Crowley states that one severe problem encountered by beginners in serious Yoga practices is the state he terms 'dryness'. The exercises become almost intolerably tedious and consequently one wonders if they lead to anything worthwhile—if, indeed, there is any point to them at all. How can this state be overcome? Or, as Crowley puts it: 'Who shall roll away the stone?' He proceeds to argue that the student should take hashish, for this will introduce him to heightened states, including—quite possibly—trances of mystical ecstasy. He will thus be convinced through personal experience that these states are both attainable and desirable. Then—and this is a key point—the student must return to disciplined practices so as to attain these states without the use of drugs. In the remainder of the essay, Crowley analyses and classifies the various states of heightened consciousness and trance, using the precise terms of Buddhist psychology, after which he appeals to men of science to research the matter.

It has been objected that drug-induced states cannot be identified with those attained by 'pure' and 'godly' mystical disciplines. But this position is intellectually sloppy and untenable. Success in magical and mystical practices does not depend on anything as vague and woolly as the favour of some divine being. For what *is* a mystical state? It is the experience of heightened consciousness accompanied by emotional exaltation, and is brought about by chemical changes in the brain and body. These chemical changes can be induced by the disciplines of Magick and Yoga—and it should be self-evident that they can also be brought about by chemicals, i.e. appropriate drugs.

Since this is the case, why not just take drugs? Why bother with the frequently excruciating labours of Magick and Yoga? Here Crowley's position has usually been grossly misinterpreted. Although he certainly encouraged experimentation with mind-changing substances, he insisted on the vital importance of disciplined work—and with good reason.

To take an analogy, let us compare a mystical experience to being at the summit of Mount Everest. Getting there through LSD is like ascending in a helicopter, standing at the peak for a few hours and then descending in a helicopter. You have had a great experience; you have admired the view; but you have certainly not climbed Mount Everest, and though your trip may have convinced you that it is worth climbing, you are no more than a vulgar day-tripper. That is a summary of Crowley's position at the time of writing 'The Psychology of Hashish'.

There are those of our contemporaries, including distinguished men of science and learning such as Doctors Leary, Lilly and R. A. Wilson whose experimental work has prompted them to argue for a modification of this position. (Indeed, during the 1960s, Dr Leary was of the opinion that sensible use of LSD would be sufficient to advance the evolution of human consciousness, though he subsequently took a more cautious view of the matter.) It is cogently proposed that the *combination* of drugs and disciplines is the most effective way of achieving the goals of Magick and Yoga. Interestingly enough, there is apparent support for this view in *The Book of the Law:* 'To worship me take wine and strange drugs whereof I will tell my prophet, & be drunk thereof! They shall not harm ye at all. It is a lie, this folly against self.'

155

Crowley came to modify his earlier views in the light of this passage and subsequent experience.

His later research was not just confined to hashish. He claimed—probably rightly—to have introduced the use of anhalonium to Europe and it was served in a libation bowl during the Rites of Eleusis at Caxton Hall in 1910. This substance is a derivative of the peyote cactus, though these days the most commonly known derivative of that plant is mescaline. Possibly Crowley did introduce Aldous Huxley to this drug in Berlin; possibly not. But certainly the latter's experience of mescaline led to his able and highly influential essay on the subject, *The Doors Of Perception.*

During his American sojourn of 1914–19, Crowley wrote a short, terse article called 'Cocaine'. And during his time at Cefalu, he took a wide variety of drugs—opium, cocaine, hashish, ether and, less happily, heroin—and meticulously analysed their effects upon his consciousness in his *Diaries*, which provide the researcher with invaluable data. His opinion, as expressed therein and also in *Liber Aleph* (written 1917–18), is that specific drugs should be used for specific purposes. Ether, for example, is the most intellectual of drugs and stimulates one's powers of analysis, so one might take it in order to reason one's way through a problem from every point of view without any emotional interference. But to inhale it when the intention was sexual would be pointless and stupid. Cocaine can speed up mental activity and temporarily fortify and enflame powers of determination, concentration and will; but anyone who sniffs it in order to experience visions or depth of feeling will be deservedly disappointed.

Contrary to popular opinion, cocaine—like hashish/marijuana, mescaline and LSD—is not physically addictive. Nevertheless, it has frequently been termed 'psychologically addictive' or 'habit forming'; and there is no doubt that excessive abuse of the substance leads to erosion of the mucous membrane, hysterical behaviour and even temporary psychosis. However, Crowley did not regard these facts as any sort of argument for legal intervention. In his view, now deriving from *The Book of the Law*, free men and women could take drugs with physical and psychological impunity. Only slaves to the sin-complex, those riddled with guilt, ran any danger of addiction and he had no pity for them at all. As *The Book of the Law* states:

> Pity not the fallen! I never knew them. I am not for them. I console not: I hate the consoled and consoler.
>   I am unique , a conqueror. I am not of the slaves that perish. Be they damned and dead! Amen. . . .

But this led to severe problems for Crowley when he finally realized that he was physically addicted to heroin.

In the view of the present writer, there is no point at all in taking this nauseating substance; and there is no point at all in punishing those who do. The original use of heroin—a principal active ingredient of opium—was as a pain-killer and to relieve the tortures of asthma: here it was and is highly effective. Otherwise it does little except poison the body, dull the mind, erase the emotions, sap the will and kill the spirit. In *Diary of a Drug Fiend*, a popular novel written in 28 days, Crowley used his own unfortunate experience as he addressed the subject.

The plot is quite simple. A man and a woman meet and enjoy a wonderful time together as they imbibe vast quantities of cocaine. They go on to take vast quantities of heroin. At first they delight in it, then they become addicted. The ecstatic thrill of their early experience degenerates into a sordid nightmare of hysteria, ruin and despair. At last it seems that the only possibility open to them is suicide (one recalls Sid Vicious and Nancy Spungen). But at this point King Lamus—a Crowley self-portrait—persuades them to come to the Abbey of Thelema ('Telepylus' in the novel). There they learn the meaning of the Law of Thelema, healthy living, self-discipline and libertarianism and this enables them to discover their respective True Wills. Although they continue very occasionally to take heroin for pleasure, the man and the woman are wholly cured of their addiction, they have found their true purposes in life and they go on their way rejoicing.

Diary of a Drug Fiend is no literary masterpiece, as its author fully realized. But it is an interesting story which contains gems of wisdom and some intriguing opinions. Of particular relevance here is the cure for heroin addiction which Lamus/Crowley advances. The addict must endeavour to discover his or her True Will by means of Magick and/or Yoga. During this time one can take as much heroin as one chooses, whenever one chooses—but there is a vital rule. Every dose must be recorded and, with it, *the reason for taking the dose.* At the end of each day, the record must be analysed. It will usually be found that every conceivable reason or excuse is given, many of them contradictory—e.g., the addict might take a dose at 3.00 pm because he felt bad and at 4.00 pm because he felt good. This is evidence of the mind playing tricks in order to subvert the True Will. Yet in order to realize the True Will—and it is hardly anyone's True Will to be a junkie—one must master one's mind. Hence the vital importance of mind-training practices; these develop Will. Lamus/Crowley insisted that as the process continues, the addict will find more and more of the recorded reasons for taking heroin to be fatuous and an infuriating impediment to the evolution of the Self. Less and less heroin will be taken. Eventually, there will no longer be an addict but a free human being.

This is all very well—but does the method work? To my knowledge, we only have Crowley's record. He used his own methods in an endeavour to cure his addiction, yet as we have seen, he suffered from the severe handicap of asthma. Nevertheless, as soon as he discovered an alternative remedy for his affliction—a legal German medication—he liberated himself from his bondage to heroin.

Unfortunately, when the German medicine was no longer available, heroin was once again prescribed for him. There was no more effective way of relieving asthma at that time and so, as hostile commentators never tire of reminding us, he died a junkie. This does not invalidate his method of curing addiction. Given the deeply disturbing epidemic of heroin abuse among the young today—a horrifying waste of national potential—one would like to see the method tried. Only when there is sufficient data will it be possible to formulate a balanced judgement as to its efficacy.

Crowley's views on drugs can be summarized as follows:
1. Drugs are tools for the exploration and enhancement of consciousness.

2. Their use can also be very pleasurable.

3. Each drug should be employed for a specific purpose and used with intelligence and will. Moreover, if the purpose is anything other than purely hedonistic, the dose and the results should be recorded.

4. All drugs should be legal for all adults.

5. Abuse of drugs is foolish but the harm done can be remedied if there is sufficient will-power.

6. An intelligent use of chemical substances directed by the will can assist the evolution of human consciousness.

8

Astrology, Qabalah and Tarot

Crowley has often been called 'the century's greatest scholar of occultism'. What exactly is 'occultism'? The word 'occult' means simply 'hidden'. The terms 'occultism' or 'the occult' have been used to mean 'hidden knowledge', although nowadays most of this 'hidden knowledge' is readily available in specialist bookshops and even large, respectable booksellers often have an openly displayed 'occult' section. The definition 'hidden knowledge', which used to be true in the days when the Church persecuted those with enquiring minds, is therefore out of date. For the last hundred years or more, the ruling intellectual establishment has not openly persecuted those who pursue 'occultism'; it has ridiculed or ignored them. The definition which will serve us best in consequence is that of an historian of ideas, the late James Webb: 'The occult is rejected knowledge.' So Crowley was a scholar of knowledge rejected by the intellectual establishment of his time and ours. Three branches of this knowledge which he studied and to which he contributed are Astrology, Qabalah and Tarot.

'I do not believe that there is one fraction of one per cent of truth in Astrology,' Crowley said to John Symonds and Rupert Gleadow towards the end of his life. He was, of course, joking; and since Gleadow was an astrologer, he was being provocative in the hope of striking up a stimulating conversation. He had in fact been casting horoscopes for most of his adult life.

Astrology is the belief that there is an intimate connection between the lives of human beings and the positions of the planets and stars. A horoscope is a diagram showing these positions at a particular moment in time, usually the moment of a particular person's birth. Astrologers argue that if this diagram is rightly understood—and this understanding, they claim, is based upon a body of knowledge which goes back hundreds if not thousands of years—one will (a) be able to make accurate statements about the character of the person involved and (b) be able to make accurate predictions about the life of that person.

Crowley insisted that the only scientific way of testing this contention is to learn how to cast and interpret horoscopes and then to cast and interpret hundreds of them, keeping a record of one's accuracy or lack of it. The mechanics of casting a horoscope are relatively simple. One requires the time and place of birth of the person involved, a set of astronomical tables for the relevant year and a method of drawing the diagram (there are a number of ways, which can be consulted in the innumerable books on the subject). Interpretation is a much more complex matter. Contrary to the laughably superficial impression given by our popular newspapers, one's 'Sun Sign' is just one fact among very many. When we say: 'Bill is an Aries,' this means that when Bill was born, the Sun had the constellation of Aries behind it when viewed from the Earth. According to astrologers, this gives us information about Bill's character: but since there are twelve constellations where the Sun could be, it gives us the same information about roughly one twelfth of the human race. The astrologer must therefore interpret the positions of the Moon, Mercury, Venus, Mars and all the other planets of the solar system. He or she must also interpret the 'aspects' or angles of all these planets in relation to one another. There are further equally important but more complex considerations which lie beyond the scope of this work. In common with other astrologers, and almost all of those who have given the matter impartial investigation by means of experimentation, Crowley argued that Astrology works—that it achieves the goals which are claimed for it.

How come? How can there be a connection between the lives of human beings and the positions of the Sun, Moon and planets? Unfortunately, nobody really knows. There are two hypotheses.

162

One is that just as the Moon, for instance, affects the tides and also human behaviour in ways we do not comprehend—according to police statistics, thefts of female underwear from washing lines show a dramatic increase on nights of the full moon; nor should we forget the etymological derivation of the word 'lunacy'—so the other planets affect us in mysterious ways, possibly through gravitation or as yet unknown magnetic fields.

The second hypothesis derives from the writings of Carl Jung and particularly from his notion of synchronicity. Proponents of this view admit that there is no *causal* connection between planetary movements and Mankind. They argue, instead, that everything in the Universe is connected with everything else: so at the moment x is born, the positions of the planets happen, among many other things, to reflect and portray the character and destiny of x.

Certainly these hypotheses—with which the present writer is not entirely satisfied—will be dismissed as nonsense by rational-humanist intellectuals. But perhaps they should bear in mind an interesting definition of an intellectual as one who declares: 'That's all very well in practice—but how will it work in theory?' The fact remains that those who take up the serious practice of Astrology conclude that it works—for whatever reason—and this phenomenon itself requires an explanation. I look forward to a time when the subject can be impartially investigated by men and women of science; and so did Crowley.

Far too many astrologers bring the subject into disrepute and ridicule because they are incapable of clear reasoning, logical scrutiny and coherent writing. This can hardly be said of Crowley's essays on *Uranus* and *Neptune*, matters on which there is little else that is worth reading. Every proposition Crowley advances is supported by the citation of numerous case-studies. For example, if he makes a statement about the effect of a certain planetary configuration, this is backed up by many examples taken from the lives of famous people, living and dead, whose horoscopes he has cast and examined. The essays on Astrology in *Magick Without Tears* clearly express his intellectually tenable approach to the matter. His principal contribution, then, was to bring the sorely required methods of logic and science to

163

Astrology. This had not been seriously attempted since that pioneering work, *Propaedeumata Aphoristica* by Dr John Dee, which was written in 1558, well before the Scientific Revolution and which, interesting though it is, could hardly convince the modern reader.

One hopes that Crowley's approach will eventually become the rule for astrologers: for the alternative is a jumble of illogical, unscientific, unsupported and insupportable assertions.

What is Qabalah? One could do worse than give the answer of the late Dame Frances Yates:

> The word means 'tradition'. It was believed that when God gave the Law to Moses he gave also a second revelation as to the secret meaning of the Law. This esoteric tradition was said to have been passed down the ages orally by initiates. It was a mysticism and a cult but rooted in the text of the Scriptures, in the Hebrew language, the holy language in which God had spoken to man.

During the Renaissance, Qabalah became an integral part of what was earlier termed The Occult Philosophy, and it is perhaps helpful to remind the reader of certain relevant tenets.

1. All is a Unity, created and sustained by God through His Laws.
2. These Laws are predicated upon Number.
3. There is an art of combining Hebrew letters and equating them with Number so as to perceive profound truths concerning the nature of God and His dealings with Man.
7. According to the Qabalah, God manifests by means of ten progressively more dense emanations: and Man, by dedicating his mind to the study of divine wisdom, by refining his whole being, and by eventual communion with the angels themselves, may at last enter into the presence of God.
9. The Universe is an ordered pattern of correspondences: or as Dr Dee put it: 'Whatever is in the Universe possesses order, agreement and similar form with something else.'

We will recall, too, how Mathers welded together Renaissance occult philosophy, including and especially the Qabalah, with certain of its sources in the creation of the Golden Dawn system.

However, the practical use of Qabalah by Magicians and Mystics has still to be defined and in *Seven Seven Seven*, Aleister Crowley gives the most succinct answer ever written:

Qabalah is

(a) A language fitted to describe certain classes of phenomena and to express certain classes of ideas which escape regular phraseology. You might as well object to the technical terminology of chemistry.

(b) An unsectarian and elastic terminology by means of which it is possible to equate the mental processes of people apparently diverse owing to the constraint imposed upon them by the peculiarities of their literary expression. You might as well object to a lexicon or a treatise on comparative religion.

(c) A system of symbolism which enables thinkers to formulate their ideas with complete precision and to find simple expression for complex thoughts, especially such as include previously disconnected orders of conception. You might as well object to algebraic symbols.

(d) An instrument for interpreting symbols whose meaning has become obscure, forgotten or misunderstood by establishing a necessary connection between the essence of forms, sounds, simple ideas (such as number) and their spiritual, moral or intellectual equivalents. You might as well object to interpreting ancient art by consideration of beauty as determined by physiological facts.

(e) A system of omniform ideas so as to enable the mind to increase its vocabulary of thoughts and facts through organising and correlating them. You might as well object to the mnemonic value of Arabic modifications of roots.

(f) An instrument for proceeding from the known to the unknown on similar principles to those of mathematics. You might as well object to the use of $\sqrt{}$, -1, x^4 etc.

(g) A system of criteria by which the truth of correspondences may be tested with a view to criticizing new discoveries in the light of their coherence with the whole body of truth. You might as well object to judging character and status by educational and social convention.

The basis of the system is a diagram called the Tree of Life. This is a multi-purpose map. It can be used to classify states of consciousness, deities, colours, plants, jewels, the physical body, or anything else in the Universe. It is a unifying symbol which embodies the entire cosmos.

It begins with Nothing, which is termed Ain. Ain is unknowable, unthinkable and unspeakable. To render itself comprehensible to itself, Ain becomes Ain Soph (Infinity) and then Ain Soph Aour (Absolute Limitless Light), which concentrates itself into a central dimensionless point. This Point is called Kether and it is the first Sephirah of the Tree of Life. The Light proceeds to manifest in nine progressively more dense emanations down to the tenth and final Sephirah, Malkuth, the physical world. This, then, is how the Universe manifests, or how God or the Goddess Nuit manifests, or how Light becomes Life—whichever words are preferred—and it is held that every set of phenomena follows this pattern. This is why the Tree of Life is viewed as a multi-purpose map.

Our map so far consists of ten Sephiroth. These Sephiroth are connected by twenty-two Paths which express the relations between the Sephiroth they connect. The original creators of the Qabalah attributed the twenty-two letters of the Hebrew alphabet to these Paths.

This system has been further expanded and made more complex over the centuries. It is held by most Qabalists that there are Four Worlds, or dimensions of existence, and each World has its Tree of Life. Many go further and work with a system whereby each Sephiroth contains a Tree, giving us a total of a hundred Trees, or if we bring in the Four Worlds, four hundred. These complexities are beyond the scope of this work. The subject can be studied with advantage in *A Garden Of Pomegranates* by Israel Regardie and/or *The Mystical Qabalah* by Dion Fortune.

It should be added, however, that there are two ways of regarding Qabalah. The traditionalists believe that the Tree of

Life is the framework of the Universe. Crowley disagreed and commented acidly: 'It was as if some one had seriously maintained that a cat was a creature constructed by placing the letters C.A.T. in that order. It is no wonder that Magick has excited the ridicule of the unintelligent, since even its educated students can be guilty of so gross a violation of the first principles of common sense.' (*Magick: In Theory and Practice*) His point was that the Tree of Life is a *classification* of the Universe, not a thing in itself. Its unique advantage, or so Crowley and other Qabalists insist, is that it is the most useful tool of universal classification which the mind of Man has ever invented.

During the 1890s, Mathers proceeded to write Tables of the Tree of Life in order to classify his occult knowledge (Dr Wynn Westcott probably assisted him) and these Tables were circulated among Inner Order initiates, including Allan Bennett. Bennett was an excellent Qabalist in his own right and Crowley learned from him, then acquired his own experience. A most fruitful result was the publication in 1909 of *Seven Seven Seven*, the classic dictionary of correspondences. As Crowley wrote in his Preface: 'The following is an attempt to systematise alike the data of mysticism and the results of comparative religion.'

Further: '... for us it is left to sacrifice literary charm, and even some accuracy, in order to bring out the one great point. This: That when a Japanese thinks of Hachiman, and a Boer of the Lord of Hosts, they are not two thoughts, but one.'

The main Tables are based on 32 numbers; that is, the ten Sephiroth and twenty-two Paths. If we look at the correspondences pertaining to the number 5, for example, we will find that the planet is Mars, the Hebrew name is Geburah (Strength), the colour for magical use is scarlet, the Element is Fire, the Egyptian God is Horus, the Greek God Ares, the Roman God Mars, the Hindu deities Vishnu and Varruna-Avatar, the stone is the Ruby, the plants are oak, nux vomica and nettle, the animals (real and imaginary) are the Phoenix, the Lion and the Child, the metal is iron, the perfume is tobacco and so on. One uses *Seven Seven Seven* to set up magical ceremonies, to guide one in meditation and to compare systems of symbolism. Once its basic principles are comprehended, one can classify new knowledge, as

167

Crowley continued to do throughout his life. His work here, based as it was on that of the Golden Dawn and Bennett, has yet to be surpassed and far too many subsequent writers have plundered it without acknowledgement.

We must now briefly turn our attention to what is known as The Literal Qabalah, the ways of 'combining Hebrew letters and equating them with Number so as to perceive profound truths concerning the nature of God and His dealings with Man'. There are three main methods: Gematria, Notariqon and Temurah. Gematria is the art of discovering the secret sense of a word by means of the numerical equivalents of each letter. As Regardie states in *A Garden of Pomegranates:* 'Its method of procedure depends on the fact that each Hebrew letter has a definite numerical value and may actually be used in place of a number. When the total of the numbers of the letters of any one word were identical with that of another word, no matter how different its meaning and translation, a close correspondence and analogy was seen.' Regardie gives an interesting example. The Hebrew for 'Serpent' adds to 358 and so does the Hebrew for 'Messiah'. This may initially appear suprising but close inspection and a further operation of Gematria will clarify the matter. For what is the Serpent? As Regardie puts it: 'The Serpent is a symbol of the Kundalini, the spiritual creative force in each man which, when aroused by means of a trained will, re-creates the entire individual, making him a God-Man.' And the Messiah is a God-Man. Furthermore, if we add up the digits 3, 5, 8, we obtain 16, and if we look up the correspondences of the sixteenth Path in *Seven Seven Seven* we find Dionysius the Redeemer. Another correspondence is that of Parsifal, who becomes able to perform the messianic miracle of redemption. As Regardie rightly states: 'We thus see the specific analogy between the words 'Serpent' and 'Messiah' which the Qabalah has been able to reveal.'

Notariqon consists essentially of constructing a new word from several words by taking the initial letters of the latter and combining them. In Temurah, the letters of a word are transposed according to various systems to form a new word. These practices concentrate the mind and are believed by their exponents to reveal truths.

Crowley made two invaluable contributions here. One is his brilliant if somewhat complex *Gematria*, published in *The Equinox* and subsequently in *The Qabalah of Aleister Crowley*; and the other, also published in the latter volume, is *Liber D. Sepher Sephiroth*, a dictionary of Hebrew words arranged according to their numerical value. As he himself described it: 'This is an Encyclopaedia of the Holy Qabalah, which is a Map of the Universe, and enables man to attain Perfect Understanding.' It is the standard work of reference for Magicians and Qabalists. As he further states in *MAGICK: In Theory and Practice:* 'Such knowledge as we have got is of a very general and abstruse, of a philosophical and almost magical character. This consists principally of the conceptions of pure mathematics. It is, therefore, almost legitimate to say that pure mathematics is our link with the rest of the universe and with "God".'

The student of Qabalah will find valuable assistance throughout Crowley's writings. The best introduction to Qabalistic studies consists of the relevant essays in *Magick Without Tears*. More advanced aspirants will be able to learn from the conceptions succinctly, if abstrusely, expressed in *Magick: In Theory and Practice* and *The Book of Thoth*. It should be stressed that Qabalah is usually found meaningless and even absurd by those with no practical experience of the subject. One cannot learn Qabalah simply by reading about it any more than one can learn chemistry without ever entering a laboratory and performing an experiment. Understanding depends entirely upon, and grows with, honest work.

The Tarot is a pack of 78 cards. There are four suits: Wands, Cups, Swords and Disks. Each suit consists of cards numbered from Ace to Ten and four Court Cards: the Knight (formerly called the King); the Queen: the Prince (formerly called the Knave); and the Princess (formerly called the Page). Our ordinary playing cards derive from the Tarot. There are also 22 'Trumps', numbered cards with curious pictures and titles like 'Death', 'The Devil', 'The Sun', 'The Star', 'The Hermit' and 'The Lovers'. These are numbered from I to XXI apart from the first card, 'The Fool', which is numbered 0 and has survived in our modern playing pack as The Joker.

The origins of the Tarot remain a mystery. Ancient Egypt, Sumeria, Morocco and even India have been suggested. It has been proposed that a group of sages or an individual sage wished to express wisdom in symbolic pictures which would survive the centuries. Possibly so, but all we know for certain is that the Gypsies brought the cards to Europe at some unidentifiable point prior to the fourteenth century and employed them for purposes of fortune-telling. In the late eighteenth century, French occultists claimed to discern hidden significance in the Tarot and its occult wisdom was insisted upon in the nineteenth century by Eliphas Levi and then by Papus (Gerard Encausse) in his *The Tarot of the Bohemians*. There are few who find the work of Levi and Papus on this matter to be particularly helpful nowadays, but Levi's writings undoubtedly influenced both Mathers and Crowley. The Tarot played a vital part in the Golden Dawn system. Aspirants learned the significance of its symbolism and also how to divine with it, in addition to its employment for exploration of what some would term 'the Collective Unconscious' and others 'the Astral Plane'. The Golden Dawn taught that the Tarot was an exposition of the Qabalah.

This assertion has been disputed from two perspectives. One body of opinion deplores all departures from the orthodox Hasidic tradition and ignores the counter-argument that the Qabalah is an evolving tool, intrinsically capable of almost infinite expansion. Others have denied all connection between Qabalah and Tarot on the grounds that there is no proven connection between the Jewish creators of the Qabalah and the Gypsies.

It cannot be proved but it can be suggested that Qabalah and Tarot shared a common origin in ancient Egypt. The symbol of the sphinx on the Wheel of Fortune Trump in the medieval packs, long before the sphinx was known in Europe, makes this plausible in the case of the Tarot. As for the Qabalah, it is believed to have originated with Moses, who received his education in Egypt and who, according to *The Bible*, became a most formidable Magician. More research on the origins and travels of the Gypsies is obviously required here in order to test this hypothesis.

Certainly, those who deny any connection between the Qabalah and the Tarot have rarely done any practical work with either. For the Tarot and the Tree of Life fit together so neatly. It will be recalled that there are ten Sephiroth and four sets of ten cards numbered from 1 to 10. There are twenty-two Paths and twenty-two Trumps. There are Four Worlds of the Qabalists and four suits and four Court Cards. Qabalah begins with 0—so does the Tarot with The Fool numbered 0. One could adduce many other considerations and continue at intolerably wearisome length, citing parallel after parallel; and opponents of this position have yet to explain these parallels sensibly. But the central point is that those who work with both Qabalah and Tarot find the connection to be self-evident and say with Crowley: 'The only theory of ultimate interest about the Tarot is that it is an admirable symbolic picture of the Universe, based on the data of the Holy Qabalah.' (*The Book of Thoth*)

In common with the Tree of Life it portrays, the Tarot is a multi-purpose tool and a multi-faceted map. Many get to grips with Qabalah through the Tarot rather than vice-versa. For example, in Qabalah the seventh Sephirah is Netzach, the tenth Sephirah is Malkuth, and these are connected by the twentieth Path, which expresses the relations between them. How is one to comprehend the nature of this relation? A pure Qabalist would study the meaning of the Hebrew letter Qoph, starting with the English translation 'Back of head', which clearly refers to the cerebellum or primitive, reptile brain and all that this implies, together with its numerical value of 100—a number which has a variety of correspondences. One who approached the matter via the Tarot would study the Tarot Trump numbered XVIII, The Moon, to which the Path is attributed, and may find that the visual symbol grants greater comprehension than intellectual abstractions. Obviously a capable seeker after wisdom would study the matter from both aspects.

The Golden Dawn also applied the 22 Tarot Trumps to Astrology and attributed them to the 12 astrological signs, and the 7 planets and 3 original elements of Fire, Air and Water— corresponding to the three Gunas of the Hindu system expounded in *The Bhagavad-Gita*—according to the system of the Ancients. Again, those who use these attributions claim that they fit neatly into a coherent order and that they work.

It was, of course, the Golden Dawn which taught the Tarot to Crowley. His first attempt to write logically on the matter was called simply *Tarot Divination*. For once he disgraced himself as a writer, for this monograph, which does not contain a single original thought, is a flagrant and shameless plagiarism from a dull and uninspiring earlier work by Mathers. The same can hardly be said of *The Wake World*, published in *Konx Om Pax,* which is a beautiful, enchanting and uncharacteristically gentle fairy tale. Lola Daydreams—or the human soul—is led by her Fairy Prince—or Holy Guardian Angel—through a series of Palaces and Ways—or Sephiroth and Paths—from idle thoughts and sleepy behaviour—Malkuth—to full consciousness of her own divinity in marriage to her prince—Kether—and her experiences and adventures on these Ways/Paths are portrayed by the Tarot Trumps.

Crowley's eventual conception of the Tarot was heavily influenced by his visions of the Trumps as living beings in the Sahara in 1909, as recorded in *The Vision and the Voice*. Further visions in *The Paris Working* (1914) augmented his comprehension of aspects of certain Trumps. Over the next twenty years and more, he became increasingly dissatisfied with the existing packs and expositions of their meaning and use. There was, furthermore, a technical problem. *The Book Of The Law* declares on the Tarot: 'All these old letters of my books are aright; but **צ** is not the Star. This also is secret; my prophet shall reveal it to the wise.'

In other words, the Hebrew letter Tzaddi and the Path to which it is attributed do not correspond to the Trump numbered XVII, The Star, contrary to Golden Dawn teaching. This created a perplexing problem. If Tzaddi was not The Star, what was? After many years of patient but futile work, he at last hit upon the solution and referred Tzaddi to the Trump numbered IV, The Emperor; and The Star he henceforth attributed to the Hebrew letter Heh and the corresponding Path. Certainly this change is logical and makes absolute sense in terms of the system. It has been found to be a perfect move which reveals truths by those who have worked with it, although a number of older Magicians and those who follow them have chosen to remain with the Golden Dawn position. This work is hardly the place for entering into the argument.

Balance and fitness were precisely what Crowley wanted in any exposition of the system of the Tarot. He also desired to create a pack which embodied the doctrines of *The Book of the Law* and his life-time of study and experience in working with the cards. Strangely enough, it seems that he made no attempt to paint his own pack. Possibly he had tired of painting; or perhaps he lacked confidence in his abilities to do justice to the matter. His problem was at last solved by his meeting with Lady Frieda Harris, who thought him the most wonderful man she had ever met. Together, and over a period of many wearisome years of arduous work, they created *The Book of Thoth.*

Crowley designed the 78 cards and Frieda Harris was the Artist Executant. The forty cards of four suits numbered from 1 to 10 consist of abstract paintings constructed so as to convey the energy named in the titles of the cards. The Court Cards and the Trumps are symbolic, figurative paintings. 'Yet the burden was sore: the anticipated three months' work extended to five years.' Crowley was a harsh task-master and on occasion forced Lady Harris to paint the same card as many as 8 times until he was satisfied. Yet for her part, Frieda could be equally demanding. 'She accordingly forced him—the laziest man in three continents!—to undertake what is to all intent an original work, including the latest discoveries in modern science, mathematics, philosophy, and anthropology; in a word, to reproduce the whole of his Magical Mind pictorially on the skeleton of the ancient Qabalistic tradition. He accepted this colossal burden; it renewed his energy and enthusiasm.' (Bibliographical Note to *The Book of Thoth.*) The work was finally completed in 1944.

Today there are far too many Tarot packs; the vast majority have been created by people who are utterly clueless (there are even singular exercises in fatuity such as 'The James Bond Tarot'). One can dismiss most Tarot decks as wholly worthless to any logical mind with the slightest aesthetic sensibility, apart

173

from four which require brief mention. The Marseilles pack has at least the virtue of several hundred years of tradition. The nineteenth-century Tarot of Oswald Wirth, a refinement of the Marseilles deck, was at least created by an artist who knew Eliphas Levi and it was commended by Papus. The Waite/Rider pack, painted under A. E. Waite's direction by Pamela Coleman Smith, has at least the advantage that Waite was taught by the Golden Dawn; but although it is probably the most widely known, it is terribly tame and twee. The Golden Dawn pack, painted by Robert Wang and supervised by Israel Regardie, is faithful to Order symbolism but in artistic terms, it is regrettably vapid. It is very hard to understand why any genuine student of Tarot should choose to work with any pack other than that of Crowley and Harris. Here every line, every colour and every symbol is included for a specific reason guided by a central purpose and—one should add—so is every brush stroke. It is a great achievement.

At the same time Crowley wrote the accompanying *Book of Thoth*, commenting with mock modesty: 'The accompanying booklet was dashed off by Aleister Crowley without help from parents. Its perusal may be omitted with advantage.' In fact, *The Book of Thoth* is 287 pages long in my edition and is easily the finest written work available on the Tarot. Most writers on the subject make unsupported, arbitrary assertions and then compound their folly by moralizing. Admittedly, there are a few decent little books which can assist the reader to tackle the complexities of Crowley's work. *The Tarot Revealed* by Eden Gray is suitable for novices. *The Tarot* by Paul Foster Case is a good, basic introduction provided that Case's occasional moralizing is ignored. But probably the best work for the beginner is a wholly unpretentious American volume called *Tarot For The Millions* in the 'For The Millions' series. These books should clarify the elements of the matter and enable the interested reader to approach *The Book of Thoth* with basic knowledge and confidence.

In the first part, Crowley sets forth his theory and principles, explaining why the pack has been designed as it has. In the second, he expounds the symbolism and meaning of each of the

22 Trumps, adding an Appendix which contains relevant visions and extracts from his writings. The third part analyses the nature of the Court Cards. Each of the 40 'Small Cards' receives scrupulous attention in the fourth part. There is then an Invocation and Mnemonics—a short and simple way of remembering the essential meanings of the Trumps—and finally, Appendices, which give a system of divination, Tables of Correspondences and other gems of occult wisdom. The system is utterly logical and coherent, despite its dazzling complexity, and a towering intellectual feat.

The truth of the above statement can only be fully comprehended through practical work with the Tarot. One has to experience the cards as living beings—*Alice In Wonderland* is not a bad analogy—and there are a number of methods by which one can accomplish this. There is, for instance, a very loose form of meditation which can help. The student simply concentrates on a given card, scrutinizes its symbolism, reflects on the meanings and correspondences of the symbols, and observes which trains of thought pass through the mind.

The following and rather more advanced practice should under no circumstances be attempted unless the student can perform The Lesser Banishing Ritual of the Pentagram—a simple ceremony available in any worthwhile magical textbook—with which the operation *must* begin and end. For a principal purpose of the Pentagram ritual is to prevent the occurrence of the principal danger of this exercise: obsession. Fortunately, it is virtually impossible to succeed in this operation without some previous experience in the training of the mind, but even so, sloppy technique usually results in unhealthy and unbalanced thought and feeling. The procedure is as follows:

1. Perform the Lesser Banishing Ritual of the Pentagram.
2. Sit up straight in a hard-backed chair facing East. Breathe slowly, deeply, regularly; and let the mind be calm.
3. Close the eyes and picture the Tarot card selected.
4. Imagine that it is on a door.
5. Imagine yourself going through that door. (This is usually the principal difficulty.)
6. Be continuously aware of your resulting experience—it is

rather like a dream—and believe nothing. It may even seem as though you are encountering noble and splendid beings who have messages of great import for you; but it is equally possible that you are just exploring the contents of your unconscious and any great 'revelations' are simply you chattering to yourself.

7. Either the experience will come to an end naturally—i.e. you will wake up as from a dream; or you will choose to end it by withdrawing through an imagined door and imagining yourself back in a hard-backed chair.

8. Perform the Lesser Banishing Ritual of the Pentagram.

9. Immediately write down your experience.

10. Check the symbolism in *Seven Seven Seven* or a similar work. If all you saw and heard corresponds, you have had an experience which has increased your understanding of the Tarot card involved.

11. If your data does not correspond—if, for example, you used The Hermit but the dominant colour was bright yellow—you have been engaged in worthless mental drifting.

The third and the most popular method of becoming familiar with the Tarot is Divination, which should not be confused with vulgar 'fortune-telling'. Once again, the clearest exposition of the theory of Divination is by Crowley:

1. We postulate the existence of intelligences, either within or without the diviner, of which he is not immediately conscious. (It does not matter to the theory whether the communicating spirit so-called is an objective entity or a concealed portion of the diviner's mind.) We assume that such intelligences are able to reply correctly—within limits—to the questions asked.

2. We postulate that it is possible to construct a compendium of hieroglyphs sufficiently elastic in meaning to include every possible idea, and that one or more of these may always be taken to represent any idea. We assume that these hieroglyphics will be understood by the intelligences with whom we wish to communicate in the same sense as it is by ourselves. We have therefore a sort of language . . . better still is the analogy between the conventional signs and symbols employed by mathematicians, who can thus convey their ideas perfectly

176

without speaking a word of each other's languages.

3. We postulate that the intelligences whom we wish to consult are willing, or may be compelled, to answer us truthfully. (*Magick: In Theory and Practice*)

Unfortunately, the method given in *The Book of Thoth* and deriving from the Golden Dawn is lengthy, cumbersome and unlikely to achieve anything for the novice. Here, therefore, is a short and simple technique:

1. Think of a question. It can be as vague as: 'What are the general developments in my life over the next month?' It can be highly specific. Frame it clearly.

2. Shuffle the cards while concentrating exclusively on the question. If you are divining for another, then that person performs the mechanics.

3. When you have done with shuffling—go by feeling here—concentrate hard on the question one final time and cut with the left hand.

4. Lay out the cards as follows:

```
          3
   1      5      2
          4
```

The fact that certain cards may be reversed plays no part in this method.

5. (1) is the influence coming into the matter. (2) is the influence in the process of departing from the matter. (3) is the most immediately apparent or conscious influence. (4) is the hidden, latent influence or subconscious factor. (5) is the key binding it all together.

6. Begin by interpreting with a work of reference which gives you the divinatory meanings. With practice, you will need it less and less.

7. Write down the interpretation as a series of statements.

8. When sufficient time has elapsed, mark your work for accuracy or lack of it. Let us say you have written ten statements.

177

Has each statement turned out to be true or false? Give yourself 1 for true and 0 for false. Tot up the marks at the end and express it as a percentage. At the end of, say, a year, average your percentages.

9. Do not be discouraged if your record of accuracy is initially poor. In the case of one diviner known to the present writer, a year's sincere, patient effort yielded a miserable mark of 35%. A year later he achieved 85% and a year after that, 92%.

10. Do not fake your record in order to impress your acquaintances for you will only be cheating yourself and this may lead to the Tarot cheating you.

We may leave the subject of the Tarot with Chapter 78 of Crowley's *The Book Of Lies:*

WHEEL AND—WOA!

The Great Wheel of Samsara.
The Wheel of the Law (Dhamma).
The Wheel of the Taro.
The Wheel of the Heavens.
The Wheel of Life.
All these Wheels be one; yet of all these the Wheel of the TARO alone avails thee consciously.
Meditate long and broad and deep, O man, upon this Wheel, revolving it in thy mind!
Be this thy task, to see how each card springs necessarily from each other card, even in due order from The Fool unto The Ten of Coins. Then, when thou know'st the Wheel of Destiny complete, mayst thou perceive THAT Will which moved it first. (There is no first or last). And lo! thou art past through the Abyss.

Too many practitioners of occultism have brought the subject into a richly deserved disrepute. Small wonder, then, that 'the occult is rejected knowledge.' Yet if the arts and sciences of occultism are pursued sensibly, it may well be found by the intelligent that here we have magnificent tools for the investigation of Man, the Universe and Man's place in it. If this does indeed turn out to be the case, full credit must be given to the splendid intellectual reformation of occultism by Aleister Crowley.

9

The Way of the Tao

... As I trod the trackless way
Through sunless gorges of Cathay,
I became a little child.
By nameless rivers, swirling through
Chasms, a fantastic blue,
Month by month, on barren hills,
In burning heat, in bitter chills,
Tropic forest, Tartar snow,
Smaragdine archipelago,
See me—led by some wise hand
That I did not understand.
Morn and noon and eve and night
I, the forlorn eremite,
Called on Him with mild devotion,
As the dew-drop woos the ocean.

The above quotation from *AHA* illustrates the impact of China upon Crowley. He was profoundly impressed also by Chinese philosophical thought during his travels there in 1905–6. He took up the study of those two great classics, *The Tao Teh Ching* and the *I-Ching*, and they became a source of strength, wisdom and inspiration for the remainder of his life.

The Tao Teh Ching is at least 2,500 years old. It consists of 81 short chapters containing aphorisms or 'strands of thought'. Traditionally, its authorship has been ascribed to Lao Tzu, although this has been disputed by some modern scholars. On

181

first reading, one can be forgiven for wondering: what on earth is this? And what in the name of Heaven does it mean? Clearly there is *some* vital significance in it, or humanity would not have continued reading it for two and a half millennia, nor would mystics, scholars and artists have consistently praised its worth. But it cannot be denied that initially one feels like echoing a previously quoted line from Crowley: 'It's rather hard, isn't it, sir, to make sense of it.'

According to Dr E. V. Rieu—an impeccable Western scholar of the Chinese language and translator of the Penguin Classics edition (one which is especially notable for its pure poetry)— those who perceive mystical significance in *The Tao Teh Ching* have been wasting their time and making fools of themselves. Dr Rieu insists that the work is merely a political treatise which recommends meekness as the proper means of survival. He deplores ignorance of the Chinese language which, he declares, has led the misguided to perceive ideas which are not there.

With all respect to Dr Rieu, he has failed to consider certain essential questions. If *The Tao Teh Ching* is merely a work which recommends meekness, how come that something so dismally dull has survived for two and a half thousand years? How come the work provides the foundation for *Chinese* schools of mystical thought? How come that Chang Tzu, one of the greatest of all sages, lauded and praised it? (Perhaps Dr Rieu would suggest that he was ignorant of his own language?) How come the Ch'an Masters of China and the Zen Masters of Japan have always extolled *The Tao Teh Ching* above all other written works? And finally, how come that the mystical content of the work is obvious to anyone with experience of these matters even in Dr Rieu's scholarly translation?

Many have declared *The Tao Teh Ching* to be the greatest book in the world. What is it about? We find no difficulty with the word 'Ching': this can be translated as 'book' or 'classic'. But 'Tao' and 'Teh' present almost insoluble problems. How can one describe 'Tao'? Unfortunately one cannot, and this is made clear by the opening statement. Here I shall quote from two translations:

The Tao described in words is not the real Tao. Words cannot describe it. (F. J. MacHovec)

The Tao that can be expressed is not the Everlasting Tao.
The Name that can be named is not the Everlasting Name.
(Dr Isabella Mears)

Close study of the text reveals that Tao cannot be declared either by speech or by silence. It is beyond both. No attempt to express its nature can possibly succeed, for it is beyond all human comprehension. Any definition, in whatever form, by definition limits it and therefore fails. Nevertheless, *The Tao Teh Ching* recommends that we have union with this Tao we cannot express, for all proceeds from it. If we have union with this inexpressible, inconceivable, incomprehensible Tao, all is as it should be.

In writing of this matter, one is painfully conscious that even if one's words are coherent, one is nevertheless writing nonsense. Nevertheless, one is irresistibly reminded of the Zen proverb: 'Teaching is like pointing a finger at the moon. The student should look at the moon and not at the finger.'

'Teh' is a word which involves one in similar difficulties. Yet *The Tao Teh Ching* offers us a clue in terms of its structure. The first part, which concerns Tao, appears to state that we should become one with it. The next part, which concerns Teh, recommends practical courses of action or non-action. Perhaps, therefore, Teh is how Tao expresses itself.

Some justification for this view will be found if we turn to the symbol created by Chinese philosophers and sages to express Tao Teh—the Yin-Yang. This consists of a circle equally divided by a serpentine curve into black and white portions. The black portion (Yin) and the white portion (Yang) together express the nature of the manifested Universe. There is continuous interplay between them. Yang, for instance, is male, fire, positive, dominant and Yin is female, water, negative, yielding and the constant interplay between Yin and Yang is the nature of all. Yang and Yin are the pairs of opposites into which all phenomena can be divided. Here one cannot resist recalling a quotation from *The Book of the Law:* 'For I am divided for love's sake, for the chance of union.'

This is spoken by Nuit, who is Infinite Space and the Infinite Stars thereof; the parallel conception of the Qabalistic Ain has been noted; and the attentive reader may already have observed the essential similarities (identity) between the conceptions Nuit, Ain, O—and Tao.

What needs to be stressed about the Yin-Yang symbol is that it is not a *rigid* division into pairs of opposites: the Chinese perceive these opposites as flowing into one another in a constant interchange of energies. This is why there is the white spot of Yang at the centre of Yin and the black spot of Yin at the centre of Yang. Once one has grasped the nature of this symbol, it becomes easier to understand *The Tao Teh Ching*. It recommends that one should become aware of the Yin-Yang within oneself and in the Universe, balance the Yin and the Yang within and without oneself and go with it, flow with it as if one were water seeking its level. This is why the Way of the Tao has been described as 'the art of doing everything by doing nothing'.

There is a simple experiment which anyone can try in order to gain greater comprehension of this notion, and here I am indebted to Mr Peter Carroll, author of *Liber Null/Liber Nox*, who has, *inter alia*, brought his studies in chemistry at the University of London to the consideration of non-rational states of consciousness. My version of his experiment is a paraphrase:

1. Lie on the floor. Do nothing. Stay there.
2. Do not get up until and unless it is necessary.
3. 'Necessary' is a word applying to anything in your life which has to be done to further your survival. You will need to exercise natural functions. You may need to eat or drink. You may have to write business letters or travel to paid employment or meet friends and acquaintances. Do that. And as soon as the task is done, return to lying on the floor and do nothing.
4. If nothing is necessary, continue to lie on the floor, even if some days pass. If you are possessed by the urge to exercise your mind or body—for instance, to paint a picture—do so. But do not move unless you or something within you deems it essential.
5. Naturally—and by now this should go without saying—record the results of this practice. It is possible that you may find

184

that many of your actions are wholly unnecessary and of no discernible benefit to you.

This simple experiment might conceivably convey an idea of Tao Teh in a way which words cannot.

The Tao Teh Ching begins with aphorisms which point to how one may become one with, and so—Tao. It goes on to recommend practical courses of conduct in a wide variety of situations—Teh. One who is in accordance with Tao will manifest Teh in all matters, great and small, from the governance of a kingdom to 'the nice conduct of a clouded cane'. For he will have Yin and Yang in perfect balance, and Yin and Yang will manifest, not *by* the self, but *through* the self. This endeavour to express the inexpressible is obviously inadequate. One can only exhort the reader to turn to the original work.

There are very many translations, a number of which appal scholars and are consequently suspect. However, a hint on approach may not go amiss. The interested reader is invited to note the similarities between the Way of the Tao as manifested in the action of Teh and the knowing and doing of the True Will; for this is what Crowley perceived. The Way and the Will are Tao Teh.

The Tao Teh Ching is not to be confused with the superstitious practices of the Chinese peasantry, which are often called 'Taoism' but which have little or nothing to do with the exalted conceptions of the book. And although *Taoist Yoga, Alchemy and Immortality* by Charles Luk is a repository of techniques which derive from centuries of thought on practical matters by Taoist sages, it should be treated as an interesting manual on a branch of Yoga and no more.

Crowley's understanding of the highest intricacies of Chinese thought—China is, after all, the world's oldest continuous civilization—was greatly augmented by his study of, and workings with, the *I-Ching, The Book of Changes*. It is said that Confucius declared that had he another fifty years to live, he would devote each day of each year to study of the *I-Ching*. This is a remarkable way of comprehending the world and it appears to derive from Taoism. It begins with the Yin and the Yang. Yin is symbolised by a broken line – –, and Yang by a straight line —.

Yin and Yang, the broken line and the straight line, are how the Tao Teh manifests. The Chinese sages proceeded to construct a system based on Yin-Yang interaction: 8 'trigrams', the 8 possible ways of putting together 3 lines from the straight and the broken. Since these 8 symbols were insufficiently complex to render a detailed understanding of universal phenomena, they multiplied the system into 64 symbols, created through combining the original 8 trigrams with the same 8 trigrams in combinations of 6 lines, which they called 'hexagrams'. In other words, there are 64 possible ways of combining a straight line and a broken line in symbols of 6 lines. This is the basis of the *I-Ching*.

If one wishes to consult the *I-Ching*, one asks a question and, while concentrating upon it, performs a mechanical operation. This involves the throwing of coins whereby 'heads' stands for Yang and 'tails' for Yin or the traditional manipulation of yarrow stalks. This gives one either a particular hexagram or the addition of special points to note and reference to a second hexagram into which the matter changes. One then takes up an *I-Ching* text; there are many versions. The text consists of 'The Title', 'The Decision', 'The Commentary', (by the Duke of Chou, a disciple of Confucius), sometimes unnecessary commentaries by subsequent editors, and 'The Image'. 'The Image' is precisely that. But accompanying it, there is a comment declaring how 'the superior man' would act. 'The superior man' is one in accordance with Tao.

Those who use the *I-Ching* find it to be extraordinarily wise and helpful in the conduct of life and this was certainly the case with Crowley, who consulted it consistently and often daily. It became his guide, philosopher and friend and he endeavoured to marry himself to the wisdom contained therein. Nor was he the only great Westerner to extol its virtues. Carl Jung gave to the *I-Ching* an honour and respect similar to that of Crowley and, with Richard Wollheim, was responsible for a laudable and widely known edition. But perhaps the most interesting reaction to the *I-Ching* is that of the mathematician and philosopher, Leibniz.

Leibniz invented binary mathematics. Before his innovation, mathematics was conducted on the basis of the decimal system, from 1 to 9 and then 10, as in the Qabalah. Leibniz sought to express all notions of Number through the use of just two symbols, 1 and 0. At the time it was possible to deride this as a useless game, for it had no practical application, though this is of no concern to the pure mathematician. When Leibniz was introduced to the *I-Ching*, he instantly perceived that the system was predicated on binary mathematics, the broken line and the straight line, 0 and 1—a system which he thought he had discovered independently. The attentive enquirer will no doubt have realized that the 'useless game' of Leibniz was what made the computer possible. Computers function on the basis of 1 and 0; if it were straight and broken lines it would be the same. This is why those whose absorption in the discoveries of science and the developments of mathematics goes hand in hand with a love of wisdom, tend to perceive the *I-Ching* as a universal computer.

Aleister Crowley sought to comprehend and express the Way of the Tao in a number of his writings. *Thien Tao*, for instance, published in *Konx Om Pax*, is a delightful tale about a kingdom in decay. A Taoist sage is appointed to remedy the situation. He succeeds through rectification of imbalance. For instance, whores and rakes are commanded to practise a period of chastity; debauchery is ordered for the prudish; businessmen have to lead a bohemian life-style, while artists must for a period practise impeccably respectable social behaviour; the obsessively clean are forced to get dirty while daily baths are compulsory for the lax. After a period of this, each one knows the pairs of opposites, the Yin-Yang balance is restored and each one is enabled freely to choose the most natural course of action. As a result of the contentment of the individuals who comprise it, the kingdom flourishes.

'Whatever Lao Tzu said and meant, this is what I say and mean,' Crowley declared aggressively in the Introduction to his 'translation' of *The Tao Teh Ching,* done in 1917. Here Crowley endeavoured to demonstrate the essential identity of Taoism and Thelema as passive and active modes of the same thing. His work can hardly be called a translation. He did not speak, write or understand the Chinese language. Instead, he took the scholarly translation of Legge and rewrote it in the light of his own comprehension. In the opinion of the present writer, he displayed greater understanding of the book's meaning and expressed it more clearly than anyone else. It is unfortunate, however, that he did not bring his poetic gifts to the work of transliteration and so although his work is outstanding, one cannot help feeling that it could have been better still.

In his version of the *I-Ching*, he tried to reduce the matter to its barest essentials but the work is not as satisfactory as one would hope. Some find that the Crowley version strikes straight to the heart of the matter. Possibly so; but the present writer finds it too lean and sparing and others have confessed their disappointment. Nevertheless, it can safely be recommended; and so can a simple, straightforward Penguin, *How To Consult The I-Ching* by Alfred Douglas.

What cannot be faulted, however, are other of his works which are relevant here. He managed the difficult and remarkable feat of equating Chinese conceptions with the Qabalistic Tree of Life in a manner which makes absolute sense and sheds new light on both. This equation was published in *The Book of Thoth*. Tao is equated with the Qabalistic Ain (0 or Nothing or Nuit). Tao manifests as Tao Teh—the Qabalistic Kether—the Point—or in terms of *The Book of the Law*, Hadit. The second Sephirah, Chokmah, masculine, is equated with Yang. The third Sephirah, Binah, feminine, is equated with Yin. United, Yang and Yin, Chokmah and Binah, manifest as all created things. There is an Abyss between their union and comprehension of its meaning by the mind of humankind.

In this Abyss, all is confusion. The Qabalists symbolized this confusion by positing the existence of an eleventh Sephirah which they called Daath, which means 'knowledge' but is in practical terms the False Crown of False Knowledge which must be transcended if one is to pass through the Abyss. Once this schema is accepted, the Chinese system fits neatly. If we take the eight possible combinations of three straight and broken lines and begin with three straight lines to symbolise masculinity gone mad in the false crown of false knowledge which is Daath, the other seven trigrams slot into the remaining seven Sephiroth of the Tree of Life.

Contemplation of this equation makes one wonder whether

the Chinese and Qabalistic systems of thought reflect the structure of the mind, and to what extent the structure of the mind reflects the structure of the Universe.

An interesting perspective on magical and mystical matters is to be found in an essay, 'The Three Schools Of Magick', published in *Magick Without Tears*. Crowley claimed, for reasons best known to himself, that the author was a journalistic acquaintance called Gerard Aumont, though as Regardie points out in his Introduction to the best edition of this work, the identity of the real author is obvious. According to the essay, there are three schools of thought concerning the nature of human existence, classified as the Black, the White and the Yellow. (One can attribute Black to Binah, the White to Chokmah and the Yellow to Kether under the Qabalistic system.)

The Black School—and here the term 'Black' has nothing to do with 'Black Magick' but is merely a category of classification— holds that Existence is Suffering. That is its fundamental axiom from which all else is deduced in the way of thought, feeling and conduct. Here we will obviously and by definition find Buddhists, who propose to deal with this axiom via the Noble Eightfold Path; Muslims, who bear this burden of the Will of Allah (kismet) by dint of sheer manhood; and, on a much lower level, Christians, who propose to solve the problem through the cowardly doctrine of vicarious atonement—to which an honest Muslim could only respond by saying: 'Jesus died for somebody's sins but not mine.' (The words are those of the musician and lyricist, Patti Smith.)

The White School holds that Existence is Joy. As Nuit declares in *The Book of the Law:* 'I give unimaginable joys upon earth: certainty, not faith, while in life, upon death; peace unutterable, rest, ecstasy; nor do I demand aught in sacrifice.' And as Hadit states: 'Remember all ye that existence is pure joy; that all sorrows are but as shadows; they pass and are done; but there is that which remains.' Thelema is the paramount example of the White School, but one clearly discerns its doctrines also in the Tantrics, Hindu and Buddhist, and in the genuine Sufis.

The Yellow School holds that Existence is Existence. This is what *The Tao Teh Ching* expresses. Masters of this school are sublimely indifferent to phenomena. They are beyond any and all considerations of Sorrow and Joy. They can be troubled only by lack of appropriate balance between Yin and Yang.

Crowley's initial approach was Black School (one recalls his struggles with the sin complex and his ensuing period as a Buddhist). It was Black School philosophy which made him reject *The Book of the Law* for five years. With the acceptance of the Book, he became the leading proponent of White School philosophy and practice and remained so until his death. Nevertheless, he was strongly drawn to the Yellow School from the moment he encountered its teachings. He revered and respected its *modus operandi*, learned from it, and, as he grew older, increasingly manifested its manner.

To clarify this statement further: his existence was conducted on many planes of consciousness as he climbed up and down the ladder of selves, which ladder is within each one of us. Sometimes he was the man, Aleister Crowley, a curious combination of gentleman and bohemian, holy man and rake-hell; yet a poet, a scholar and an outstanding sportsman. Sometimes he was Perdurabo, Ceremonial Magician of the Golden Dawn; or Baphomet, Grand Master of the OTO Sex Magicians. Sometimes he was the Master Therion, the Great Beast 666, Prophet of the New Aeon which will endure for roughly two thousand years; and sometimes he was a Taoist sage, wholly unconcerned about trivial time-scales.

His popular novel *Moonchild*, written in 1917, demonstrates his attitude in a simple, comprehensible fashion. There are two characters based on Crowley: Cyril Gray, the dynamic, young Adept; and Simon Iff, the middle-aged Master. At one point in this continuously entertaining thriller, Gray and Iff are attacked by a Black Magician who sends to their garden a filthy, slobbering demon. Cyril Gray proposes a counter-attack with pentagrams, hexagrams and other weapons of the White School armoury; but Simon Iff walks out into the garden, exudes love so as to equilibriate the hatred sent forth, and thus absorbs the demon into his being, rather as a child might gobble up jelly, to the great discomfiture of the enemy who sent it.

This is the Way of the Tao. To put the matter in terms of

martial arts, the Taoist warrior never finds it necessary to strike a blow. His art consists of putting into the mind of his potential opponent the idea that it would be distinctly foolish to attempt any attack.

Moonchild is also notable for Crowley's later perception of Allan Bennett, who appears as an honoured minor character. The tone suggests that Bennett proceeded from the Black School to the Yellow. The account of Bennett on his return to London in the early 1920s given by Clifford Bax in *Some I Knew Well,* would appear to confirm this view. Certainly *Moonchild* demonstrates Crowley's veneration for Bennett as a Master of the Yellow School.

In *The Great Beast* John Symonds recorded his opinion that in old age, Crowley had metamorphosed from Pan into the Devil, and he added: 'The Devil is always a gentleman.' Symonds was perhaps seeing that which he most desired to see—as was so often the case with those who met Crowley. However, if we ignore childish considerations of sin, guilt and infantile wish-fulfilment and turn instead to the last writings, *The Book of Thoth* and *Magick Without Tears,* we find not the Devil but a Taoist sage. In what is probably his most perceptive comment on Crowley—whose *Diaries* display a testy impatience with a dull disciple—Kenneth Grant stated that for the former, the Way of the Tau (the magical Phallus) led to the Way of the Tao.

The paradoxes of existence and of Crowley's own nature were probably best enunciated in *The Book of Lies.* This is a unique work of 91 short chapters of aphorisms or 'strands of thought', which seeks through the art of paradox to express the inexpressible and, like *The Tao Teh Ching,* to touch the heart of so many varied modes of mystical, magical, human and practical endeavour. It is Zen—originally a Japanese formalization of the Chinese marriage between Tao and Buddhism—which has in this century sired a number of increasingly informal ways to wisdom. A contemporary Western Adept of Zen—some would say a Master—Dr Robert Anton Wilson is responsible for the delightful and truthful aphorism: 'It's not true unless it makes you laugh.' For laughter is a sublimated orgasm—and simultaneous orgasm between Yin and Yang, Binah and Chokmah and Nuit and Hadit brings forth all created things. Perhaps this is why Taoist and Zen Masters are celebrated for their constant laughter. For in addition to gems of practical magical wisdom, *The Book of Lies* contains some of the wittiest and most hilarious metaphysical passages ever written. One can only exhort the reader to turn to it.

The Tao cannot be stated, it can only be shown. And so it is probably best to end this chapter on a serious note, though it contains its share of humour, by quoting Chapter 13 of *The Book of Lies*, 'The Wanderings or Falsifications of the One Thought of Frater Perdurabo Which Thought is Itself Untrue':

PILGRIM-TALK

O thou that settest out upon The Path, false is the Phantom that thou seekest. When thou hast it thou shalt know all bitterness, thy teeth fixed in the Sodom-Apple.

Thus hast thou been lured along That Path, whose terror else had driven thee far away.

O thou that stridest upon the middle of The Path, no phantoms mock thee. For the stride's sake thou stridest.

Thus art thou lured along That Path, whose fascination else had driven thee far away.

O thou that drawest toward the End of the Path, effort is no more. Faster and faster dost thou fall; thy weariness is changed into Ineffable Rest.

For there is no Thou upon That Path: thou hast become The Way.

10

From Neophyte To Ipsissimus

Suppose one wished to try the system of magical attainment set forth by Crowley as the A∴A∴ way. What would be required?

Crowley's method consists of a series of ascending Grades. It is proposed here to explain their nature according to the essay published as an Appendix to *MAGICK: In Theory and Practice*, 'One Star In Sight' (though *Liber XIII: Graduum Montis Abiegni*, 'an account of the task of the Aspirant from Probationer to Adept', published in *The Equinox* and *Gems From The Equinox*, is also relevant).

The first Grade is that of Student. His business—and one trusts that one will be forgiven for not writing 'his or her' whenever there is a possessive pronoun—is 'to acquire a general intellectual knowledge of all systems of attainment'. To this end, there is a reading list consisting of magical, mystical and philosophical classics. Naturally this includes *The Equinox, The Tao Teh Ching, The I Ching, The Upanishads, The Bhagavad-Gita, The Dhammapada, The Oracles of Zoroaster, The Divine Pymander* of Hermes Trismegistus, *The Golden Verses of Pythagoras* by Fabre d'Olivet and other essential classics. But rigorous logical thought is also stressed with the inclusion of Thomas Paine's *The Age of Reason*, Frazer's *The Golden Bough*, the *Essays* of Hume and T. H. Huxley, Berkeley's *Three Dialogues* and Kant's *Prolegomena*. There is also a supplementary reading list of relevant fiction.

The object of this course of reading is to familiarize the student with all that has been said by the Great Masters in every time and country. He should make a critical examination of them; not so much with the idea of discovering where truth lies, for he cannot do this except by virtue of his own spiritual experience, but rather to discover the essential harmony in these varied works. He should be on his guard against partisanship with a favourite author. He should familiarize himself thoroughly with the method of mental equilibrium, endeavouring to contradict any statement soever, although it may be apparently axiomatic.

The general object of this course, besides that already stated, is to assure sound education in occult matters, so that when spiritual illumination comes it may find a well-built temple. Where the mind is strongly biased towards any special theory, the result of an illumination is often to inflame that portion of the mind which is thus overdeveloped, with the result that the aspirant, instead of becoming an Adept, becomes a bigot and a fanatic. (Appendix I: *Magick: In Theory and Practice*)

The intellectually enlightened Student then proceeds to the next step, that of Probationer. Although in the period 1909–13, A∴A∴ under Crowley as V.V.V.V.V. did hold group meetings, he subsequently turned against the idea. He came to perceive the OTO as being the Order for group workings, while the A∴A∴ would be concerned with individual attainment. To this end, the system works on a supervisory basis, not dissimilar to that employed at the Universities of Oxford and Cambridge. For all practical, magical purposes, the aspirant is in contact only with a supervisor in the Grade above him and a pupil in the Grade beneath him. The Probationer, therefore, is supervised by a Neophyte, the next Grade, and in turn supervises a Student. Nor can one proceed to a higher Grade until one has prepared one's pupil to advance also.

That is how Crowley intended the Order to work. In practice, the rule was often broken and this is still the case. For example it is thought that an Adept cannot deny supervision to a Probationer solely on the grounds that circumstances of time and place have rendered a chain of strict hierarchical communication impossible. There has to be some flexibility according to the factors involved: but what follows is how Crowley ideally wanted the system to work.

The task of the Probationer is 'to begin such practices as he may prefer and to write a careful record of the same for one year'. On the face of it, this sounds laughably easy. In fact, only a minority survive the course. Their intention arouses every manner of opposition, both within and without themselves.

One who is tough enough to continue becomes a Neophyte, which corresponds to the tenth Sephirah of Malkuth. The principal task here is 'to acquire perfect control of the Astral Plane'. In order to succeed, the Neophyte will have to acquire a fair mastery of basic magical technique and of basic yoga practices, for on one level 'perfect control of the Astral Plane' means perfect control of the imagination and unconscious. At this point, exams come into it. He is tested in 'the Spirit Vision' or 'Astral Journeying' by giving him a symbol unknown and unintelligible to him, and he must interpret its nature by means of a vision as exactly as if he had read its name and description in the book when it was chosen.

There are other tasks of each Grade which lie beyond the scope of this work.

As will probably have been discerned, the system of the A∴A∴ is somewhat more demanding than that of the traditional Golden Dawn. The Golden Dawn required—and still does—magical learning and evidence of practice, together with the passing through of a series of initiations. One who succeeds can be initiated as a Golden Dawn Adeptus Minor. Yet even after this substantial achievement, a Golden Dawn Adeptus Minor may not be able to pass the Neophyte examination of the A∴A∴.

If the Neophyte does so, he becomes a Zelator, which corresponds to the ninth Sephirah of Yesod. 'His main work is to achieve success in Asana and Pranayama.' In other words, he must become a proficient Hatha Yogi, adept in posture and breath control; and the examination is hardly easy. 'In examination for physical practices, there is a standardised test. In Asana, for instance, the candidate must remain motionless for a given time, his success being gauged by poising on his head a cup filled with water to the brim; if he spill one drop, he is rejected.'

'He also begins to study the formula of the Rosy Cross.' That is to say, he studies the basics of Sex Magick; and the energies of Kundalini, the Serpent Power at the base of the spine aroused by the Zelator's practices, will have given him insight.

Yesod corresponds to sexuality and imagination. The next stage, corresponding to the eighth Sephirah of Hod, which relates to intellect, is that of Practicus who 'is expected to complete his intellectual training, and in particular to study the Qabalah. He will then be fitted to pass the required test.

'In intellectual questions, the candidate must display no less mastery of his subject than if he were entered in the "final" for Doctor of Science or Law at a first class University... In the Qabalah, the candidate must discover for himself, and prove to the examiner beyond all doubt, the properties of a number never previously examined by any student.' In the words of another system, he must become adept in Gnana Yoga.

In the next Grade of Philosophus, which corresponds to the seventh Sephirah, Netzach and Emotion, the aspirant is 'expected to complete his moral training. He is tested in Devotion to the Order.' This moral training is in fact—and at last—undemanding for all who do not suffer from the sickness of guilt. 'Each member must make it his main work to discover for himself his own true will, and to do it, and do nothing else.' As for 'Devotion to the Order':

> He must accept those orders in *The Book of the Law* that apply to himself as being necessarily in accordance with his own true will, and execute the same to the letter with all the energy, courage, and ability that he can command. This applies especially to the work of extending the Law in the world, wherein his proof is his own success, the witness of his Life to the Law that hath given him light in his ways, and liberty to pursue them. Thus doing, he payeth his debt to the Law that hath freed him by working its will to free all men; and he proveth himself a true man in our Order by willing to bring his fellows to freedom.

196

The Philosophus is also expected to succeed in Bhakti Yoga, the Yoga of Love or Devotion to a Deity. *The Bhagavad-Gita* and/or Crowley's *Liber CLXXV: Astarte vel Liber Berylli* are the key works here.

There follows an intermediate Grade between Initiate and Adept, called Dominus Liminis who 'is expected to show mastery of Pratyahara and Dharana'. In other words, he must become adept in Raja Yoga and attain the trance of Dhyana.

The Grades so far described are part of what Crowley termed the 'Outer College' and in a side-swipe at Mathers, he also called it 'the G.D.'. At various points there were examinations in practical magical skills:

The power to make and 'charge' talismans is tested as if they were scientific instruments of precision, as they are... In invocation the divine force must be made as manifest and unmistakeable as the effects of chloroform; in evocation, the spirit called forth must be at least as visible and tangible as the heaviest vapours; in divination, the answer must be as precise as a scientific thesis, and as accurate as an audit; in meditation, the results must read like a specialist's report of a classical case.

Success here leads to the next Grade of Adeptus Minor (without), which corresponds to the sixth Sephirah of Tiphareth. He is 'expected to perform the Great Work and to attain the Knowledge and Conversation of the Holy Guardian Angel'. This is the climax; this is the point to which all practices have led. If the Great Work is accomplished, he knows and does his Will and as an Adeptus Minor (within) 'is admitted to the formula of the Rosy Cross on entering the College of the Holy Ghost'. That is to say that he or she is enabled to practise the highest forms of Sex Magick and becomes a member of the Inner Order which Crowley termed 'the R.C.'.

After a period of work, the next Grade of Adeptus Major follows. This corresponds to the fifth Sephirah of Geburah and here he 'obtains a general mastery of practical Magick, though without comprehension':

To attain the Grade of Adeptus Exemptus, he must accomplish Three Tasks; the acquisition of absolute Self-Reliance, working in complete isolation, yet transmitting the word of his superior clearly, forcibly and subtly; and the comprehension and use of the Revolution of the wheel of force, under its three successive forms of Radiation, Conduction and Convection (Mercury, Sulphur, Salt; or Sattvas, Rajas, Tamas), with their corresponding natures on other planes. Thirdly, he must exert his whole power and authority to govern the Members of lower Grades with balanced vigour and initiative in such a way as to allow no dispute or complaint; he must employ to this end the formula called 'The Beast conjoined with the Woman' which establishes a new incarnation of deity; as in the legends of Leda, Semele, Miriam, Pasiphae, and others. He must set up this ideal for the orders which he rules, so that they may possess a not too abstract rallying-point suited to their undeveloped states.

As an Adeptus Exemptus, the Grade which corresponds to the fourth Sephirah of Chesed, he 'completes in perfection all these matters'. He is also meant to write a thesis which sets forth his comprehension of the Universe. 'He then either (a) becomes a Brother of the Left Hand Path or, (b) is stripped of all his attainments and of himself as well, even of his Holy Guardian Angel, and becomes a Babe of the Abyss, who, having transcended the Reason, does nothing but grow in the womb of its mother.'

The plunge into the Abyss is of particular interest. As previously observed, you have to give up all that you have and all that you are. You must die in order to be reborn. This process is charmingly described by the heroine of Crowley's fairy tale, *The Wake World:*

You have to leave the House of Love, as they call the Fourth House. You are quite, quite naked: you must take off your husband-clothes, and your baby-clothes, and all your pleasure-clothes, and your skin, and your flesh, and your bones, every one of them must come right off. And then you must take off your feeling clothes; and then your idea clothes; and then what we call your tendency clothes which you have always worn, and which make you what you are. After that you take off your consciousness clothes, which you have always thought were your very own self, and you leap out into the cold abyss, and you can't think how lonely it is. There isn't any light, or any path, or anything to catch hold of to help you, and there is no Fairy Prince any more: you can't even hear his voice calling you to come on. There's nothing to tell you which way to go, and you feel the most horrible sensation of falling away from everything that ever was. You've got no nothing at all; you don't know how awful it all is. You would turn back if you could only stop falling; but luckily you can't. So you fall faster and faster; and I can't tell you any more.

There are those whose (justifiable) pride in their extraordinary attainments leads to ruin. And this, contrary to all the nonsense which has been written, is the real and crucial difference in Magick between what is called the Left Hand Path and the Right Hand Path. There are quite a number of ways by which one can reach the exalted state of Adeptus Exemptus, or Supreme Adept, or One who dwells in Chesed (Glory), or whichever terminology is chosen to describe a glorious state of being. There is no 'good' or 'bad' about methods employed; either they work or they do not. It is only at this stage of a magical career that there is a vital and essential distinction:

Below these [Black Magicians] in one sense, yet far above them in another, *are the Brothers of the Left Hand Path.* These are they who 'shut themselves up', who refuse their blood to the Cup, who have trampled Love in the Race for self-aggrandizement.

As far as the grade of Exempt Adept, they are on the same path as the White Brotherhood; for until that grade is attained, the goal is not disclosed. Then only are the goats, the lonely leaping mountain-masters, separated from the gregarious huddling valley-bound sheep. Then those who have well learned the lessons of the Path are ready to be torn asunder, to give up their own life to the Babe of the Abyss which is—and is not—they.

The others, proud in their purple, refuse. They make themselves a false crown of the Horror of the Abyss; they set the Dispersion of Choronzon upon their brows: they clothe themselves in the poisoned robes of Form; they shut themselves up; and when the force that made them what they are is exhausted, their strong towers fall, they become the Eaters of Dung in the Day of Be-with-us, and their shreds, strewn in the Abyss, are lost.

Not so the Masters of the Temple, that sit as piles of dust in the City of the Pyramids, awaiting the Great Flame that shall consume that dust to ashes. For the blood that they have surrendered is treasured in the Cup of our LADY BABALON, a mighty medicine to awake the Eld of the All-Father, and redeem the Virgin of the World from her virginity. *(Magick: In Theory and Practice.)*

If one grain of ego remains, it will be swollen out of all proportion and the result will be, not a Master, but a monster. To put it plainly, one will go mad. From one perspective, it is part of the Oath of the Master of the Temple to 'interpret every phenomenon as a dealing of the Universe with my soul'. This would include an event as mundane as viewing an advertisement on television. It is very hard to distinguish this state from that which is its parody, paranoid-schizophrenic psychosis. Perhaps our litmus-paper test should be the old proverb: 'By their fruits shall ye know them.' If the alleged Master's subsequent utterances are true, then the facts will be correct and the logic coherent. Alternatively, these utterances may be aesthetically beautiful. As Keats declared: 'Beauty is Truth: Truth, Beauty,' and according to mystics this obtains above the Abyss with the union of apparently disparent pairs of opposites. However, if there is neither fact, logic nor beauty, one can safely ascribe the utterances of the self-proclaimed 'Master' to a disorder of the mind.

The task of the Magister Templi or Master of the Temple, whose Grade corresponds to the third Sephirah Binah, is 'to tend his "garden" of disciples, and to obtain a perfect understanding of the Universe. He is a Master of Samadhi.'

Very few human beings have ever attained to the Grade of Magus, which corresponds to the second Sephirah Chokmah. Legend has it that there were eight: Lao Tzu, Siddartha (Gautama Buddha), Krishna, Tahuti (Thoth), Mosheh (Moses), Dionysus, Mahmud (Mohammed) and Perdurabo (Crowley), though it is thought that there may have been a few others who aligned their Wills with the Word of the Magi. The Magus 'attains to wisdom, declares his law... and is a Master of all Magick in its greatest and highest sense.'

The supreme Grade of Ipsissimus, which corresponds to the first Sephirah Kether, 'is beyond all this and beyond all comprehension of those of lower degrees'. In endeavouring to state something sensible, we are confronted by difficulties similar to those we encountered in considering Tao Teh. Crowley's paradox in his Commentary on Chapter 56 of *The Book of Lies* will enlighten some and confuse others: '... also "Malkuth is in Kether, and Kether in Malkuth"; and, to the Ipsissimus, dissolution in the body of Nuit and a visit to a brothel may be identical.' The reader who wishes to pursue this matter is advised to turn to the five paragraphs on The Ipsissimus in 'One Star In Sight', which contains also some interesting remarks on the system described here:

By such methods, the A∴A∴ intends to make occult science as systematic and scientific as chemistry; to rescue it from the ill repute which, thanks both to the ignorant and dishonest quacks that have prostituted its name, and to the fanatical and narrow-minded enthusiasts that have turned it into a fetish, has made it an object of aversion to those very minds whose enthusiasm and integrity make them most in need of its benefits, and most fit to obtain them.

We shall leave the subject with Chapter 6 of *The Book of Lies:*

CAVIAR

The Word was uttered: the One exploded into one
thousand million worlds.
Each world contained a thousand million spheres.
Each sphere contained a thousand million planes.
Each plane contained a thousand million stars.
Each star contained a many thousand million things.
Of these the reasoner took six, and, preening, said:
This is the One and the All.
These six the Adept harmonised, and said: This is the
Heart of the One and the All.
These six were destroyed by the Master of the Temple; and
he spake not.
The Ash thereof was burnt up by the Magus into The
Word.
Of all this did the Ipsissimus know Nothing.

11

The Prophet and the Man in the Street

It is not the Will of every man or every woman to advance along the magical Path—although as the present writer has continuously suggested, those who do so are increasing the sum of human intelligence and aiding the vital process of human evolution. Nevertheless, is the message of the Prophet, and are the ideas he enunciated, of any relevance to the man in the street? It will be argued here that they are of even more relevance to Man than to Magician, for the Law of Thelema is basically the Law of Nature: 'This shall regenerate the world, the little world my sister, my heart & my tongue, unto whom I send this kiss.'

Do what thou wilt shall be the whole of the law is obviously relevant to everyone. This commandment states that the only serious business of life is to come to know one's True Will and to do it. Everything else is a process of disconnected fatuity. The True Will can manifest itself in an almost infinite number of ways. It might be one's Will to be a carpenter, or an artist, or a doctor, a lawyer, an accountant, a businessman, a plumber; or a fine parent of a remarkable child. Unfortunately, neither our system of education nor the structure of our society presently allows for the doctrine that *Every man and every woman is a star,* with lamentable individual and social consequences. As the American novelist and philosopher, the late Ayn Rand put it: 'The hardest thing in life is doing what you really want.' *Do what thou wilt* bids water to seek its level and the Laws of Gravity to operate; it bids sheep to eat grass and wolves to eat sheep. The incompetence, stupidity, dishonesty and corruption of those who govern have rendered them incapable of perceiving something so

203

basic and simple—and the current wave of desperate violence, senseless crime and mindless cruelty can hardly surprise any detached observer.

Nor is it in the slightest degree original to remark that the planet is in crisis. This has been said by so many so often since 1904 that it is a platitude. There are a variety of causes of this disturbing situation; but one is mundane. From 1904 to our own time there has been more technological change than in the preceding two thousand years, and each year this process of change accelerates. It is very hard for those conditioned by the decayed Victorian values which somehow survived into the pre-1939 world to grasp the nature of contemporary reality. Yet they, and younger people who have aped them in the hope of political and economic advancement, hold power. One can hardly blame any sane human being for feeling that he or she is being governed by a pack of baboons.

It is quite extraordinary how difficult it is to communicate with these creatures. One states a thousand and one times that *Do what thou wilt* does not mean 'Do what you want', adding that mere wants interfere with the Will, only to be informed by them that Thelema is a 'Do what you want religion'. There is no arguing with fools. What can be done, however, is to present its politics, ethics, educational ideas, mode of worship and outlook for humankind in the hope that some people might understand plain language.

Politically, Thelema means individualistic libertarianism. Crowley began as a High Tory—one who believes that the privileges of an elite can only be balanced and must be justified by practically executed concern for the less fortunate—and ended in *Magick Without Tears* by advocating old-fashioned American Republican individualism. But there is no need to follow his example. One can be a Conservative, a Liberal, a Social Democrat, a Socialist or something not yet conceived—provided that the system proposed is advocated because it will lead to more freedom and more individualism, enabling every man and every woman to do his or her True Will.

It should be obvious from this that the idea of humanity as a bee-hive or a termite colony is anathema to all Thelemites. It should also be self-evident that all totalitarian systems such as fascism and communism are loathsome to anyone who embraces Thelema.

It may well be asked how women fit into the Thelemic vision.

'Let the woman be girt with a sword before me,' it proclaims. Moreover, 'Every man and every woman is a star.' Nor should one forget that the first chapter of *The Book of the Law* is dictated by the Goddess of 'Infinite Space and the Infinite Stars thereof'—Nuit. Woman is equal to Man in every way—though her ways may well be different—and she has no right but to do her will.

In a note published in *Seven Seven Seven*, Crowley expounded his ideas about the Will of Woman. He thought that it manifested in three ways and that the task of Woman is to discover which way and to identify with it. He categorized these ways as The Mother, The Wife and The Whore. The Mother seeks for a male who will impregnate her and guard her and the children; the man is a secondary consideration. The Wife seeks after a first-class man. The Whore enjoys herself. All are worthy of equal respect.

It is clear beyond all doubt to the present writer that Crowley omitted one vital sub-category on account of his time and his conditioning. I refer to the modern phenomenon of the Career Woman, whose central interest is her work and for whom men are sex-objects, though from time to time she may fall in love. In other words, she manifests The Whore and her behaviour is wholly in keeping with *The Book of the Law*. Crowley had little to add to these basic principles other than to state in *Magick Without Tears* and elsewhere that it was a principal task of Woman to resist and control moods, which interfere with the doing of her Will.

The ethics of Thelema can readily be understood by anyone with any notion of a code of honour: 'Beware lest any force another, King against King!' But it conflicts arise, as they are bound to do in terms of human action: 'As brothers fight ye!' The values are very similar to, if not identical with, those espoused by King Arthur and his Knights of the Round Table.

Crowley dealt with education in *Liber Aleph: The Book of Wisdom or Folly*. Here he proposed that the child should be introduced to every intellectual and athletic discipline and the resulting inclinations observed and encouraged. For, he insisted, there is no point in forcing children to learn things they do not want to learn—other than the basic essentials for survival in society which they will probably want to learn anyway. Those who show no academic potential should be taught a trade of their own choosing and allowed to leave school as early as possible, which cuts short a useless waste of time. By contrast, those who wish to pursue learning, in whatever branch, should receive every assistance.

Some thought was devoted by Crowley to the notion of popular religion. Many people seem to need it. Public rites and ceremonies appear to answer some yearning within the human psyche. For this purpose, Crowley proposed a religion based upon the facts of Nature. His central rite is the intensely beautiful *Gnostic Mass,* which exalts both the masculine principles of the Sun and its vice-regent on Earth, the Phallus; and the feminine principles of the Moon and the Sky and their vice-regent, the Vagina. In later life, he also composed rituals for a religion of Witchcraft—something which will be considered later.

The outlook for humanity, according to Thelema, remains in doubt. If Thelema is rejected and stupidity triumphs, the result will be a nuclear holocaust and perhaps, as Bernard Shaw once suggested, the planet will be turned over to the dolphins, who have greater cranial capacity. If Thelema is accepted, the results will still be deeply disturbing to any rational-humanist mind dominated by nineteenth-century conceptions—as was for a long time the case with Aleister Crowley. In the process of destruction of the Old Aeon of Osiris, there will be—and is—bloodshed and barbarism. And as everything in humanity which has been suppressed for two thousand years comes forth, the pitiless Law of Nature will prevail. After that—and only after that—will it be possible for humanity to bask in the sunshine of the Aeon of Horus, then proceed to the next evolutionary stage, which has been termed the Aeon of Truth and Justice. This is a desirable prospect, but even a cursory reading of any newspaper will demonstrate that humanity is not yet ready for this leap of consciousness and must first traverse an Aeon which involves the stripping away of the false selves we have so ignorantly fashioned and the unveiling of the true Self, naked and unashamed.

The man in the street can make a good start by advocating and practising the principles enunciated in Crowley's *Liber Oz:*

Liber LXXVII

OZ: the law of the strong: this is our law and the joy
of the world (AL.II.21.)

Do what thou wilt shall be the whole of the law (AL.I.40.)

thou hast no right but to do thy will. Do that, and
no other shall say nay. (AL.I.42–3.)

Every man and every woman is a star. (AL.I.3.)

There is no god but man.

1. Man has the right to live by his own law—
   to live in the way that he wills to do:
   to work as he will:
   to play as he will:
   to rest as he will:
   to die when and how he will.

2. Man has the right to eat what he will:
   to drink what he will:
   to dwell where he will:
   to move as he will on the face of the earth.

3. Man has the right to think what he will:
   to speak what he will:
   to write what he will:
   to draw, paint, carve, etch, mould, build as he will:
   to dress as he will.

4. Man has the right to love as he will:—

Take your fill and will of love as ye will, when, where, and with whom ye will.—(AL.I.51.)

5. Man has the right to kill those who would thwart these rights.

the slaves shall serve—(AL.II.58.)

Love is the law, love under will.—(AL.I.57.)

Aleister Crowley

PART FOUR

The Influence of the Beast

1

Disciples

It is said of Masters—proclaimed and self-proclaimed—that 'by their fruits shall ye know them.' It will therefore be instructive to inspect the fates of those who became disciples of Crowley.

Some achieved next to nothing. A good example here is the Earl of Tankerville, who originally went to Crowley because he thought he was being 'magically attacked'—whatever that may mean—by his wife and his mother-in-law. In spite of his time spent with Crowley, which included a visit to Morocco, his only legacy to posterity is a statement which Crowley was fond of quoting cheerfully: 'I'm sick of you always teaching, teaching, teaching, as though you were God Almighty and I were some poor, bloody shit in the street.'

Some came to grief. Charles Stansfeld Jones, Frater Achad—Crowley's 'magical son'—chose to exercise a pre-rogative of the A.˙.A.˙. system; when only a Neophyte, he swore the Oath of the Master of the Temple and catapulted himself into the Abyss. He did indeed discover the mathematical key to *The Book of the Law*, as that work had predicted, but afterwards seems to have gone mad. He wandered the streets of Vancouver wearing nothing but a raincoat and flashed astonished passers-by in the belief that he was dispelling 'the veils of illusion'. Subsequently, he compounded his folly in Qabalistic studies by taking the Serpent of Wisdom—a symbol which connects in due order the Paths of the Tree of Life—and turning it upside-down. In a final burst of insanity in 1948, he announced that the Aeon of Horus had been aborted after a mere 34 years and replaced by the

Age of Truth and Justice, the Aeon of Maat, the Age of Balance, yes, the Age of Aquarius, which is how that notion first came into being.

Nevertheless, it should be stated that many practising occultists find Achad's Qabalistic workings to be of value: moreover, he knew and influenced the unjustly neglected British novelist Malcolm Lowry, author of *Under the Volcano*.

Norman Mudd, Cambridge graduate and sometime Professor of Mathematics at the University of Bloemfontein, was another casualty. Although he contributed to the elucidation of many mathematical puzzles contained in *The Book of the Law*, Mudd seems to have been incapable of practising one of the Book's injunctions: 'O be thou proud and mighty among men!' Instead he was wont to introduce himself with the woeful words: 'My name is Mudd.' Eventually he committed suicide.

Others achieved more. J.F.C. Fuller, whose first book, *The Star In The West*, extolled Crowley, his poetry and his philosophy, went on to write good books called *Qabalah* and *Yoga* and to become one of the most influential military strategists of the twentieth century. He was the architect of the British victory at Cambrai (1917), where tanks were first used effectively. And in his later writings, he devised the notion which the Germans called *Blitzkrieg*—war conducted in a series of lightning strikes employing massed formations of tanks supported by dive-bombers. Unfortunately, British High Command chose to ignore his ideas; and still more unfortunately, these were eagerly adopted by the Nazis. Fuller was one of the two Englishmen invited to Hitler's fiftieth birthday celebrations. One's respect for Fuller is somewhat soured by his strong sympathy for fascism, but possibly restored by the excellent historical work he wrote after the Second World War, *The Decisive Battles of the Western World*.

When Victor Neuburg parted from Crowley, he became a delightful but utterly spineless and ineffectual hen-pecked character, skilfully portrayed by Arthur Calder-Marshall in *The Magic of my Youth*. This dismaying lack of will should not prevent one from recalling that he wrote his finest poetry under Crowley's influence—*The Triumph of Pan* (1910) is superb by any standard—and in the thirties he discovered Dylan Thomas and Pamela Hansford-Johnson.

C.F. Russell, a Crowley disciple of the Cefalu period, quarrelled with 'the old man' and returned to America to found 'the Great Brotherhood of God' in California during the 1930s—an Order which taught a type of Sex Magick. This subsequently passed into the hands of Louis T. Culling whose *A Manual of Sex Magick* has already been mentioned. Russell, who was reportedly in good health during the present writer's sojourn in California in 1981-2, was also responsible for a most eccentric autobiograpy called *Znuss is Znees* (there is a copy in the Warburg).

The laudable careers and many accomplishments of Gerald Yorke—whose reported last words were: 'Ah! Now for the Great Adventure!'—and Israel Regardie—whose heart failed after a good dinner with an old friend—have already been described.

What of the many women who came under Crowley's influence? There were those who did nothing more than sleep with him and enjoy his company; there were those who inspired important work; and there were those who found their true selves and made their own original contributions.

There is no point in citing examples of the first category; the list is too long and demonstrates merely that Crowley loved women. One wishes his critics were capable of doing the same. In the second category we find Rose Kelly, a beautiful but empty-headed woman of society who was nevertheless responsible for bringing down *The Book of the Law* through Crowley; Mary d'Este Sturges, through whom Abuldiz communicated, and who inspired *Book Four*; Leila Waddell, a remarkable violinist when she was with Crowley and a mere fiddler when she was not, who inspired *The Book of Lies*; Roddie Minor, 'the Camel', who brought to the Beast the Amalantarah communications and who inspired the works of 1917—*Moonchild, The Tao Teh Ching* transliteration and *Liber Aleph*; and Dorothy Olsen, who gave her money to his work.

In the third category, the achievements of Leah Hirsig have yet to be justly evaluated. Certainly she inspired *The Confessions*, the wisest portions of the *Diaries*, the *Commentaries* on *The*

Book of the Law and other valuable works written by Crowley during their relationship. But it is impossible to judge the work she did for herself without reading her own *Diaries*; and it is good to learn that their publication is in preparation. The letters written by Jane Wolfe to Crowley, especially those of the 1940s when she had attained to an admirable magical maturity, are also worthy of publication. There may well have been other women who benefited from knowing the Beast as he benefited from knowing them; and probably the final classic example is Lady Frieda Harris, whose finest paintings—the 78 cards of *The Book of Thoth*—were done under his direction.

One is honour bound to end this section by reminding the reader of the words of Gerald Yorke, country gentleman, county cricketer and ultimately representative in the West of the Dalai Lama; and of Israel Regardie, celebrated psychologist, author and magician: 'Everything I am today I owe to him.'

2

Magical Orders

The Golden Dawn is still in being. It fragmented after the crisis of 1900 in which Crowley played a key part. One section remained loyal to Mathers; another, under J.W. Brodie-Innes, scholar and author of the superb historical romance *The Devil's Mistress*, eventually made peace with Mathers; a third under A.E. Waite did its best work in influencing the mystic Evelyn Underhill and the extraordinary novelist, poet and scholar, Charles Williams, but otherwise degenerated into the pompous platitudes consequent upon Waite's endeavour to replace practical Magick with Christianity; and a fourth under Dr Felkin became what Francis King has aptly termed 'astral junkies'—i.e., they let their minds drift in a wholly futile search for 'supernatural masters'. Even so, Felkin did some good work. He founded a New Zealand Temple which flourishes today under the leadership of Mr Pat Zelaski. I have not met Mr Zelaski nor am I sure of how to spell his name, but those of his letters and documents which I have seen suggest a powerful, wholly sincere personality. Moreover, the English GD branch deriving from Dr Felkin's work, the Stella Matutina, continued into the 1930s when it initiated, *inter alia*, Dr E. Graham Howe, the noted psychiatrist; Professor C.D. Broad of Cambridge, philosopher and author of *The Mind and its Place in Nature*; and Israel Regardie.

Regardie proceeded to the Grade of Adeptus Minor but was disgusted by the Order's neglect of practical work, which finally provoked him into breaking his Oath of secrecy and publishing the GD teachings. He felt that if this was not done, the GD would

215

die; and he demonstrated his integrity by signing away to another any resulting financial benefits. In the opinion of the present writer, the GD would indeed have died without Regardie's courageous action in making its teachings available to all who seek wisdom; and his consistent advocacy in his many books of the classical virtues of the GD system—fully demonstrated in his final masterpiece, *The Complete Golden Dawn System of Magic*—has brought about a revival. These contemporary movements should be distinguished from surviving descendants of the original Order and it is necessary that we first take a cursory look at these.

When Mathers died of influenza in the 1917–18 epidemic, he was succeeded by his wife Moina. It has been alleged that she sold charters to American aspirants in order to raise money; I do not know whether or not this is so. What is certain is that she came to dislike intensely one Violet Firth. Ms Firth left the Order, adopted the name Dion Fortune, wrote an excellent book called *The Mystical Qabalah*, a number of very interesting novels and much journalistic slush; and founded an Order to practise GD Magic, The Fraternity of the Inner Light. After her death, this Fraternity 'christianised' and so castrated itself, though there are still some surviving members. Two noted writers on magical matters, Gareth Knight (Basil Wilby) and W.E. Butler, were disciples of Dion Fortune: their sound magical text-books are marred by irrelevant moralizing. Butler went on to play a major part in founding an Order called Servants of the Light, which exists today under the leadership of an author and ceremonial Magician, Dolores Ashcroft-Nowicki. Also worth mentioning are Robert Turner and Dave Edwards—the latter's *Dare To Make Magic* is technically sound but stylistically atrocious—whose Order of the Cubic Stone did, and possibly still does, work in the GD tradition. Such is the state of Golden Dawn Magick in the United Kingdom, though I am reliably informed that an elderly GD Adept desires to charter a new Temple for a new generation.

There are a number of GD Temples in the United States. These exist in Atlanta, Georgia; Las Vegas, Nevada; San Diego, California—and there are two rival Temples in Los Angeles. One is led by Ms Patricia Behmann, also known as Patricia Monocris and Cris Monnastre, essayist, composer, singer and student of Psychology. I have spent time with Ms Behmann, and I cannot fault either her magical sincerity or her ceremonial competence. The other Temple, under the auspices of Chris Hyatt's Israel Regardie Foundation, is led by Ms Laura Jennings, of whom the same could be said.

As can be discerned from the foregoing, Ms Behmann and Ms Jennings, who used to work together, are not the best of friends. Though I have no part in the disputes they courteously conduct, on the basis of the available evidence it would appear that Ms Jennings—a teacher of Tarot and a student of Archaeology— makes a greater endeavour to teach GD Magick without any pressure upon one's personal life (though some might dispute a contention best left to California).

Whether it is Ms Behmann, Ms Jennings or someone else who is in charge of GD Temples—and there may be others quietly pursuing their work—the attitude to Crowley does not vary. He is regarded as an excellent ceremonial Magician, an outstanding Qabalist and occult scholar, and a brilliant magical technologist. Certain of his innovations, such as the Unicursal Hexagram—a hexagram drawn in one continuous line—have been adopted. In its current forms, the Golden Dawn does not accept *The Book of the Law*; but it learns from and teaches Crowley's magical expertise.

It is the failure of the GD to accept *The Book of the Law* which has caused certain members of the OTO to declare that the former is useless for the present purposes of humanity. The GD has responded to this charge by acidly pointing out that the Ceremonial Magick which is now taught in the lower OTO degrees derives directly from the Golden Dawn—which is perfectly true, except when the innovations of Crowley are adopted. Certain OTO members try to answer this by arguing that without the Law of Thelema and the energy which is termed 'the 93 Current', the GD is no longer relevant to the present Aeon; and that the work of introducing people to the glories of Magick, formerly performed by the GD, is now done by the OTO. It is not my purpose here to embroil myself in this controversy. It remains to be seen whether the Golden Dawn will find sufficient inner strength and outer adherents to manifest successfully in the UK as an Outer College of the A∴A∴.

The A∴A∴ is currently in a period of silence. Aspirants who seek hard enough and sincerely enough, and who possess the capacity to discriminate between initiates and charlatans, will find those capable of assisting their quest.

The history of the OTO is more complex. As early as the mid-1920s, Eugene Grosche, of the German Saturn-Gnosis Lodge, declined to accept Crowley as 'World Teacher' and went his own way, though he preserved cordial relations with the Prophet. Today, the Lodge grows steadily under the author and translator, Herr Ralph Tegtmeier, whose intelligence, years of magical experience and good humour impress all whom he encounters and who openly deplores the lack of a German critical tradition of debate as he tests his ably reasoned opinions in fair argument.

The remainder of the OTO Lodges went with Crowley as Outer Head. Some work was done in California during the 1930s by Wilfred T. Smith, but it was as uninspiring as its leader's name. However, things became more interesting in the 1940s with the advent of Jack Parsons, who came to run an active California Lodge and who by profession was a brilliant rocket-fuel scientist (a crater on the Moon is named after him). Parsons also wrote a few good poems, though it seems that some of his ideas were in excess of his ability to cope with them. He endeavoured to find a Scarlet Woman so as to produce a 'Moonchild', a praeter-human intelligence born within a human body.

'I get fairly frantic,' Crowley commented morosely, 'when I contemplate the idiocy of these louts.' In view of what transpired, one can hardly blame Baphomet for his scathing remarks. For a disciple came to Parsons, begged to assist him in the 'Moonchild' working, won Parsons' trust—and then robbed him of his woman and his money. This character, who went on to make sound practical use of all he had learned, was L. Ron Hubbard, the late Founder and Godfather of a highly successful movement which suppresses individual initiative, Scientology.

Jack Parsons finally made his exit by dropping a phial of

218

fulminate of mercury and blowing himself up in his own laboratory in 1951. Those who believe in reincarnation will no doubt wish him better luck next life.

When Crowley died, his will appointed Karl J. Germer his successor as OTO Outer Head. Germer was utterly sincere and utterly impossible. He had no sense of humour at all. He refused to advance candidates through the OTO degrees, engaged in quarrels with a wide variety of people whose standards of Thelemic purity failed, in his view, to match his own, and, leaving his affairs in a mess, he died of cancer of the testicles.

Those who have studied the matter tend to agree that the succession passed to Frater Paragranus, Herr R. Metzger of Switzerland. For a time, his conduct of affairs could not be faulted. The OTO flourished and its workings received a glowing tribute from a visitor, Francis King, in his much underrated work, *Sexuality, Magic and Perversion*. Unfortunately, and for reasons best known to himself, Frater Paragranus decided that the ranks of the OTO should be open only to initiated Freemasons, with the predictable result that, by all accounts, the Lodge has shrunk into a moribund club for elderly companionship.

Another claimant of the OTO successorship is the Englishman Kenneth Grant, author of *The Magical Revival, Aleister Crowley and the Hidden God, Cults of the Shadow, Nightside of Eden* and *Outside the Circles of Time*. Mystified, one tries to read Mr Grant's books, concluding that if he wishes to conceal, he should keep silent; and if he wishes to reveal, he should learn how to write. Mr Grant was chartered by Germer to head an 'Encampment' working the first 3 degrees of the OTO 9 degree system. Although the Crowley *Diaries* of the 1940s imply that he found Grant dull but earnest, the latter did an able job until roughly 1955 when he announced his curious discovery of a 'trans-plutonian' planet, unknown to astronomers, which is apparently of cosmic mystical and magical significance. Germer expelled Grant from the OTO.

I have seen several photocopies of the expulsion notice; and have also heard it argued that Germer did not have the right to expel anybody without prior consultation with senior colleagues.

Whatever the rights and wrongs of the matter, Grant's reaction was to set up another magical Order which he called 'The OTO', to claim publicly to be the OTO 'World Head' and to receive royalties from collaborative editing ventures of Crowley material with John Symonds. It is difficult to take Mr Grant's claims seriously.

In the 1940s, the late Grady McMurtry, who became a Major in the US Army, was a pupil of Crowley, whose *Diaries* commend him. Crowley gave McMurtry a charter for emergency purposes which granted him 'Caliphate' powers. That is to say that in the event of the OTO being in danger of withering and dying, McMurtry was entitled to lead a revival as 'Caliph'. When it seemed as though this eventuality had come to pass, Major McMurtry apparently contacted Gerald Yorke and Israel Regardie—whom he regarded as 'the Eyes of Horus' and guardians of Crowley's legacy—and asked for their approval of his action in activating the powers of the Caliphate: I am reliably informed that they did indeed approve. Major McMurtry then spearheaded an OTO revival from his base in Berkeley, California, conducted the affairs of the Caliphate OTO to the satisfaction of its initiates, and died in 1985, leaving behind him a growing and fruitful organization. There are currently 45 Lodges, Oases or Camps all over the United States; 9 in Canada; 3 in Australia; 1 in New Zealand; 2 in Norway; 2 in West Germany; and 1 in the Caribbean, France and Yugoslavia; and in England there is 'The OTO Oasis', with subordinate Camps in London, York, Leamington Spa and Hastings. The Caliphate OTO publishes a journal called *The Magical Link*, certain of Crowley's works, and excellent documents of magical instruction for its members. The author of many of these latter papers is Mr William Heidrick, an American who is clearly a highly intelligent magical technologist. The present Caliph of the OTO, the Headquarters of which are now in New York City, is known as Hymenaeus Beta.

The English section of the OTO was only re-established in the Spring of 1986 by Mr David Rietti and it has grown steadily, and he has attracted a wide variety of capable and intelligent individuals to the Order.

There are a number of other magical orders and groups which exist in places as varied as New York, Chicago, Mexico City, Cincinnati, Los Angeles, San Francisco, London, Leeds, Whitby and Bristol: most are heavily influenced by the writings of Crowley.

One interesting phenomenon of the late 1960s and the 1970s was the Church of Satan led by a former carnival performer and police photographer, Anton Szandor LaVey. This organization preached enlightened self-interest, exalted the powers of the unrestrained libido LaVey termed 'Satan', and based its practical Magick on a debased and simplistic, though moderately effective, version of Crowley's writings. By the mid-1970s, this form of Satanism briefly became the fastest growing cult in the United States. Mr LaVey then appears to have lost interest in the magical aspects, which led to a breakaway offshoot, the Temple of Set under US Army Major, Michael Aquino. The documents of this Temple demonstrate Major Aquino's notable intellectual gifts but are then regrettably marred by the inclusion of a work which he claims to have received from a praeter-human intelligence. This work, which is devoid of intellectual or aesthetic merit, claims that the Aeon of Horus has already ended in favour of the Aeon of Set of which Mr Aquino is the Prophet.

One finds similar fatuity in *The Book of Maat*, 'received' by 'Sister Nema', one Maggie Crosby of Ohio. Here one learns that the future 'Aeon of Maat', the Aeon of Truth and Justice, somehow runs 'concurrently' with the Aeon of Horus. Mr Kenneth Grant nevertheless found value in Ms Crosby's work, which influenced his own, and she joined his Order for a time; though nowadays she writes well-intentioned letters and essays on occultism, feminism, socialism and being nice to one another for amateur publications. As time goes on, one can expect to see more dreary documents from alleged praeter-human intelligences proclaiming that the Aeon of the Crowned and Conquering Child has been aborted before it has properly begun in favour of something else, and which in utterly uninspiring, vapid verses hail the breathless, eager scribe—usually a dismal nonentity—as Prophet of the new New Aeon—whereupon the

Prophet deluges unfortunate readers in an ocean of unintelligible gush.

The subject of Witchcraft demands a few words and has been defined in Chapter 1 of Part 3. It is possible that there are and always have been hereditary witches, though it is impossible to establish the fact. During the 1940s, Dr Gerald B. Gardner, a retired civil servant, claimed to have made the acquaintance of a Hampshire coven of witches of hereditary persuasion—a claim supported by Louis Wilkinson (though Francis King doubts if the lineage goes back much beyond a hundred years). Dr Gardner nevertheless wrote a novel, *High Magic's Aid* and a purported work of non-fiction, *Witchcraft Today*, which insisted on the existence of an age-old and widespread cult of Witchcraft. As a result, dozens of covens promptly sprang into existence, all claiming to be survivals of this age-old cult, and so the modern Witchcraft revival came into being.

Dr Gardner gladly supplied earnest enquirers with 'original and ancient' rites and rituals of Witchcraft. These were in fact written mainly by Aleister Crowley, who had initiated Dr Gardner into the Third Degree of the OTO. For Crowley felt that if there had to be a popular religion, then some form of Witchcraft, based as it is on the principles of Nature and fertility, might be eminently suitable. Gardner tampered with these rites and rituals, mainly by introducing his private obsession with flagellation, but they are used—usually without acknowledgement or with denial of their true source—by most witches today.

During the 1960s and 1970s, the Witchcraft movement expanded on account of the activities of Alex Sanders, much of whose magical work and teaching was drawn from Crowley. A separation between Mr Sanders and his High Priestess and wife Maxine has resulted in separate organizations. These are still in being.

Modern Witchcraft, then, bears the stamp of Crowley, who also influenced the Druids—as is evidenced by the substantial correspondence in the Warburg between him and a Druid leader, MacGregor Reid.

There has recently erupted among the younger generation of Magicians a phenomenon called 'Chaos Magick'. This attempt at liberation from outmoded formulae and patterns of behaviour has manifested itself in an intriguing variety of ways. In the work of Mr Peter Carroll, author of *Liber Null/Liber Nox, Psychonaut* and a number of essays, one finds excellent sense and sometimes brilliant technical innovations. Mr Carroll does not accept *The Book of the Law* but admires Crowley as a man and as a Magician. He heads an organization called the IOT—the Illuminates of Thanateros—which used to cost one pound to join, after which one did six months' solitary magical work and kept a record before proceeding further. His partner in running the IOT is Mr Ray Sherwin but the latter's speeches and essays are unrelievedly tedious.

Chaos Magicians have a justifiably high regard for the work of Mr Lionel Snell, author of *SSOTBME*—an acronym for Sex Secrets Of The Black Magicians Exposed—*Thundersqueak: Confessions of a Right-Wing Anarchist* and other fascinating philosophical and magical essays which, among other things, display the influence of Crowley. Mr Snell, a Cambridge graduate and sometime Eton schoolmaster, is notable for his wit, his modesty and the exquisite subtlety of his reasoning.

Mr Snell is an occasional contributor to a periodical originally called CHAOS and now called KAOS, edited by a science graduate of Imperial College, London and former *Daily Mirror* journalist, Joel Biroco, originally named Steve Marshall. Mr Biroco is a powerful writer: he is responsible for the extremely stimulating pamphlet, *The Exorcist of Revolution*, and there is rarely a dull page in the journal he edits. Chaos Magicians are encouraged by him to use the space he gladly offers as a forum for discussion and debate, and although this makes for entertaining reading, one is often struck by the curious combination of revolutionary declarations, good intentions and utterly clueless lack of elementary magical technique. One has still to discover just what the term 'Chaos Magick' means. At times it promises interesting and valuable insights and innovations; at others, in other hands, it seems like a neurotic, adolescent mess.

All Chaos Magicians appear to be strongly indebted to Crowley, although some are fond of criticizing his personality and social conditioning in order to emphasize their own independence. However, the majority of youthful adherents to Thelema and Magick tend to refer to The Beast 666 affectionately as 'Uncle Aleister'.

Obviously there have been some lamentable and wretched consequences stemming from Crowley's work. A classic example is something called 'the Solar Lodge' which existed in Southern California during the 1960s and whose activities seem to have consisted of drug-taking, the burglary of magical books and documents and the physical and mental abuse of children. Unsurprisingly, Charles Manson was for a time a member of this moronic group of perverts and such techniques as he learned from them may well have contributed to his subsequent psychopathic condition.

One can hardly hold Crowley responsible for the activities of lunatics and idiots. And it is fair to state that virtually every magical organization, in an age where these are growing, owes to his work a debt which, even if unacknowledged, cannot be repaid.

3

The Arts and the Final Legacy

Crowley has featured as a character in many works of fiction: *The Magician* by W. Somerset Maugham; *The Goat-Food God* by Dion Fortune; *Casting the Runes* by M.R. James; *He Cometh and He Passeth By* by H.R. Wakefield; *The Hieroglyph* by Ethel Archer; *The Deuce and All* by George Raffalovitch; *Man Without a Shadow* (the U.S. title is *The Sex Diary of Gerard Sorme*) by Colin Wilson; *Masks of the Illuminati* by Robert Anton Wilson; and perhaps most notably, in *The Devil Rides Out* by Dennis Wheatley.

This marvellous thriller was written by a man whose knowledge of Magick consisted merely of reading a few books and having a few coversations with Rollo Ahmad, yogi and author of *The Black Arts*; the Reverend Montague Summers, author, scholar, bibliophile and pervert; and Aleister Crowley, on whom he based his villain, Mocata. Yet *The Devil Rides Out* has served the function of introducing many to Magick—a function performed in the nineteenth century by Lord Edward Bulwer-Lytton's splendid, if occasionally sentimental, romance, *Zanoni*. It is unfortunate that the late Dennis Wheatley chose to remain relatively ignorant of Magick, for he wrote other 'Black Magic' thrillers such as *To The Devil—A Daughter* which are highly entertaining. Perhaps in the future, his function will be served more adequately by Crowley's *Moonchild*.

A chapter in the novel *Jurgen* by James Branch Cabell is based on Crowley's Gnostic Mass. There are also many works of non-fiction which discuss Crowley and his work. *The Star In The*

West by J.F.C. Fuller; *Some I Knew Well* by Clifford Bax; *Laughing Torso* by Nina Hamnett; *Swordfish and Stromboli* by Denis Clarke; *The Occult* by Colin Wilson; *The Cosmic Trigger* by Robert Anton Wilson; *Seven Friends* by Louis Wilkinson; *The Magic of my Youth* by Arthur Calder-Marshall; *The Great Beast* and *The Magic of Aleister Crowley* by John Symonds; *Aleister Crowley: The Man; the Mage; the Poet* by Charles Richard Cammell; *Confessions and Impressions* by Ethel Mannin; *The Beast* by Daniel Mannix; *The Magical World of Aleister Crowley* by Francis King; *The Sword of Wisdom* by Ithell Colqhoun; *The Magician of the Golden Dawn* by Susan Roberts; *The Magical Dilemma of Victor Neuburg* by Jean Overton Fuller; *The Eye in the Triangle* by Israel Regardie; and *Hitler and the Age of Horus* by Gerald Suster.

In the 1970s Snoo Wilson wrote a play, *The Beast*, which was performed at the Shaw Theatre by the Royal Shakespeare Company, with Richard Pascoe as Crowley; and which was rewritten and revived in the early 1980s. In 1986 the Ballet Rambert performed a work called *Ceremonies* at Sadler's Wells. The score by Edward Shipley and the dances manifested the seventh Enochian Key originally explored by Crowley.

One cannot touch on the art of cinema here without praising Kenneth Anger, a practising Thelemic Magician whose extraordinarily beautiful, if disturbing, *Magick Lantern Cycle* portrays the effects of magical rituals—most notably in *Inauguration of the Pleasure Dome, Invocation of My Demon Brother* and *Lucifer Rising*. Mr Anger, an exquisite craftsman, has been quoted on the cover of *Time Out* as stating: 'The one product I'm trying to sell is Aleister Crowley.'

When we turn to music, we find of course that the Beatles put Crowley on the 'People We Like' record sleeve of their deservedly legendary *Sergeant Pepper's Lonely Hearts Club Band* album. Mick Jagger and certain of the Rolling Stones were drawn to Magick during the late 1960s—hence the album, *His Satanic Majesty Requests*, and the superb opening track of *Beggars' Banquet*, 'Sympathy For The Devil', as well as the music composed and played by Jagger for Kenneth Anger's *Invocation of My Demon Brother*. Jimmy Page of Led Zeppelin has collected Crowley material for many years and on account of his enthusiasm, purchased Crowley's former house at Boleskine. David Bowie mentioned Crowley on his *Hunky Dory* album. Ozzy Osbourne has recorded *Mr Crowley* and a 1986 poster advertizing one of his albums portrayed the Beast and the Scarlet Woman. There is a very strong Crowley influence on the music and videos of Genesis P-Orridge, leader of an organization called The Temple of Psychic Youth. In addition, one can discern the legacy of the Beast in tracks such as 'Gloria' as rendered by Patti Smith, 'Hate And War' by The Clash and 'Shake Her Shake' by The Cure. But there is no point in wearying the reader further with an interminable list of examples.

A quotation from Kenneth Grant's Preface to *The Confessions of Aleister Crowley* illustrates the unexpected way in which Crowley keeps cropping up (and Grant's statements are supported by Dr Robert Anton Wilson): 'Timothy Leary, for example, identifies himself so entirely with the current initiated by Crowley, and the "coincidences-synchronicities between my life and his", that he considers one of his aims to be the completion of the work of preparing the world for cosmic consciousness, which Crowley had begun.'

The fact remains that in England today, to take an example of an 'advanced' Western nation, there are between three and four million unemployed people, the majority of whom are under thirty; a rising tide of ignorance and illiteracy; a plague of AIDS; an epidemic of heroin addiction; an unprecedented fever of lies and corruption in politics and commerce; and a devouring wave of crime and violence which the police confess themselves unable to combat. Given the stupidity which currently dictates how things are done in our country, these facts would hardly have surprised Crowley.

There is a choice before us. We can ignore the patent facts, descend further into the mire of stupidity, and finally end the consequent misery by hurling nuclear bombs from nation to nation for no good reason, annihilating humanity and poisoning for centuries the air, water, earth, flora and fauna of this beautiful planet.

Or we can go forward to the next evolutionary stage, which

will involve the recognition of ourselves as we truly are. If we succeed in so doing, if we can utilize every atom of the corporeal, imaginative, intellectual, emotional and spiritual faculties which have enabled our species to survive all manner of historical, geographical and geological crises—then that will be the principal Legacy of the Beast.

About the Author

Gerald Suster is a writer and journalist who has studied the life and work of Aleister Crowley for many years. He is the author of *Crowley's Apprentice*, also published by Samuel Weiser, *Hitler and the Age of Horus*, a number of novels, and is the editor of the *Essential Writings of Dr. John Dee*. He lives in London.